MW00916578

Dealing with the Hand I Was Dealt

By

Brandy Hunt

Table of Contents

Introduction

Introduction

If you have ever played a card game, or watched one being played, you are aware that each player is dealt an equal amount of cards. However, none of the cards they have received are the same; nor will any of them play their cards in the order that they were received.

In the standard American 52 card deck, no two cards are identical. Consequently, no two hands will ever be identical.

While waiting for the game to begin, the players take a moment to scan their cards and make pre-game judgments. Judgments such as: "this is a bad hand," "let's just throw it in," or "I am unable to perceive how this is going to work out for me" are all comments that are blurted out from players that think they got dealt a bad hand. Judgments such as these are spoken by players that think they got a hand worth playing: "This is going to be good", "finally I got something to work with", or they may just sit in silence, not wanting to give the other players any indication that they perceive they will have the victory.

Regardless of what they think, neither party knows the end result. What some may perceive as a good hand can fail, if not played correctly. There is always the slim chance that there may be a turning point in the game for the players that did not have the top notch hand from the beginning, causing them to gain the upper hand! Whether the players like the hand they were dealt or not they will not be able to just throw away in their cards without forfeiting the entire game. Also, they cannot exchange cards until after the game begins. As those cards will be as random as the original ones received, they must keep the cards they are given, play with what they have, or forfeit the game.

In my opinion, life is very similar to a card game. Just like card players, the sequences of our cards, (life's situations) were not hand-picked by us. Most of the time our premature judgment and emotional dependency, makes us feel like we have received a losing hand. That does not mean we can or should, just throw it in and start over. We only get one life and we must deal with what we have been given. We may not get to choose the cards, but we do get to choose how we play them.

During this card game we call life; risk is a major factor when dealing with the hand you have been dealt. Nobody knows every detail of their life from A-Z. We cannot predict every outcome. If so, we would definitely choose more favorable circumstances than the ones we receive. I know I would. Often, we must make a decision based on what we are holding in our hands right now, without all the answers.

Regardless of what we believe the outcome will be, we have to play the game to the finish. I'm sure if we could pick our hands we would pick all the cards that would be guaranteed "winners". I know I would pick cards such as jokers, aces, wild cards and so on. Seldom would we pick situations that end in conflict, death, disagreement, pain or bitterness. We would only choose those things that make us feel good or show us in the best light.

We did not get to choose our parents, our background, or how we would be raised. Neither, did we have input in choosing our culture. We were exempt from choosing our cards the day they asked us how many people we would like to become friends with, or better yet enemies, and we definitely

4

were left out when questioned about the amount of adversity we would each have to endure throughout our lifetime. Where was I when my financial status or list of future accolades was being determined?

Ultimately, each one of us has been dealt a specific "hand". Regrettably, some of us have been given a more difficult hand than others.

However, I have good news my friends! It is not by our own power that we deal with this life. Did you know that God is not surprised by anything we are going through? God tells us in his word he had a plan for your hand long before you received it. As a matter of fact he planned this whole thing!

Jeremiah 29: 11 says: *For I know the thoughts that I think toward you, says the Lord, thoughts of peace and not of evil, to give you a future and a hope. NKJV*

It is exciting to know that my cards were handpicked by God. There is less pressure knowing that I am not alone and this chaos we call life has a purpose. We are all going through something we consider difficult. No one is exempt from the trials and tribulations of life.

I know it feels like trouble has access to your personal address, email address, work address, Facebook, and even your Twitter account at times, but pain does not have favorites. It will eventually impact us all.

We will all experience suffering, heartache, pain, frustration, anger and rejection without explanation. Fortunately, trouble is not forever and happiness, joy, peace, kindness, and love will all return at some point. No matter what cards you have been dealt, it is up to us to determine how we deal with them.

In "Dealing with the Hand I Was Dealt" the focus is not so much about how I came to deal with my current problems and circumstances, but how God took me back to the places where the root of the problems began. He showed me what the real issue was, and to start there, not here. Healing only came after dealing. Now I know how to properly use the hand I have been dealt to my advantage to grow, build, prosper, and ultimately discard what is not assisting me in reaching my fullest potential. Yes! Pain has purpose.

The key factor of dealing with it is to know what you are dealing with. We must identify with the original pain, hurt, or breaking point so that we can deal with it from where it began. Before you begin this healing process, one decision has to be made in order for it to be a foundation for all others. When you are truly ready to deal with the hand you have been dealt you must decide quitting is not an option!

No matter what cards you were dealt, or what chance you THINK you have of winning, I have news for you, YOU WIN! You will conquer that thing that has been holding you in bondage for so long. You will not be bound by your past mistakes, failures or setbacks any longer! In "Dealing with the Hand I Was Dealt" I will reveal very personal details about my own struggles, heart aches, tragedies, mistakes and achievements. I hope that you will be able to learn and grow from my experiences.

"How did I get here? This is the question we so often ask ourselves when we have arrived at a place in life we are not proud of. Often times I hear, as I am sure you have as well, "your decisions led you here". While a portion of that may be true, some situations may have been avoided and some situations were unavoidable. Specifically speaking, there was nothing you did to deserve your father walking out of your life, being raped, being the victim of molestation, experiencing a job loss, or the untimely death of a loved one. It is not necessarily something that we asked for but it's definitely something to be gained from it. Events happen to us daily. Sometimes quicker than we can recover from one event, we are faced with something else.

The struggle between jobs, family, career, children, husbands, elderly parents, etc. can have your head spinning out of control with all the things that can or may go wrong on a daily basis. Life can get so out of control at times and it's just not fair! At some point we find ourselves standing still or at least attempting to climb out of the chaos asking the infamous question: How did I get here? Good question.

We do a good job of going back to what happened, but never really owning up to the truth of what it has conditioned us to become. So let's be real transparent and ask ourselves the hard question: It happened, so now how am I going to deal with it? Will I just ignore it, as if it never happened? Remind yourself: If you refuse to deal with it now, you will deal with it later. Are you ready for true freedom? Are you ready to deal with the hand you were dealt?

By picking up this book, you have the opportunity to walk in victory and have the best experience of freedom you have ever had in your life. Yes it is possible! You can live free from the pain of your past! Bondage, lack, poverty and shame are not your portion! Sister, we must eliminate the pain once and for all that's causing the lack of progression in our lives. I pray that as you share in my journey from abandonment to acceptance you too will deal with the hand you were dealt with grace, peace, and joy. If by chance you are a man, or woman, who has caused trauma your child, spouse, or family, no matter the reason, call them. Share this book with them. Ask for their forgiveness and extend forgiveness to them. Throughout this journey I pray that you experience the love of our heavenly Father, Jesus Christ, like never before. The Father loves you, and so do I!

Dear Daughter,

You are healed. I wish above all things that you prosper and be in good health. The stripes I took for you on Calvary were for your healing. I was bruised so you would not have to be. I bore you iniquities so that you would not have to. You do not have to be afraid. You are a creation of faith, not fear. I am not angry with you. I love you. I have ordained you to be great. I have positioned you to be effective right where you are! Make a joyful noise at all times. Even when it gets tough, take pride in yourself. It's not being conceited to be confident about the God that lives on the inside of you. Begin to see the solution. You can walk out your destiny in full confidence knowing that I will be with you until the end. Keep your focus on the goal even if you do not see a manifestation of results. The results are coming. I promise. People might say you are not worth it and have counted you out. You might even feel as if you are not worth it. But YOU ARE WORTH IT!

Forever Yours,

Your Father

Card #1:

Dealing with Abandonment

Dealing with Daddy

Daddy Please Don't Go

My Not So Sweet 16

Fatherless Daughter

www.Foolishness.com

Dealing with Daddy

Dealing with daddy? How about dealing with no daddy? I know that's what you may be thinking. What a way to start off right? There is no way that I can soften the blow of such a tragedy. I know it is a painful subject. I know it hurts. For some, you have turned a cold shoulder to your father's absence and have managed to live your lives without him. Sadly, this is for many, where it all began.

Think for a moment back to your 8 or 9 year old self. What are your thoughts about your father then? Is it pain or joy? Continue to venture on to when you became angry or disappointed with your father. Maybe all you have ever known was his picture. That's a very painful memory to carry with you. That is the day your life, changed, forever. The day you realized he was never coming back. Also, if you have never known him, you started out with pain, abandonment, and rejection, which for you is a normal feeling, no big deal right? Wrong. It is the biggest deal of your life and if not dealt with it will spill over into EVERY area of your life. You will become the thing you hate the most. Abandonment and rejection found a seat in your heart, and to this day they still reside there. They feel as if they have a right to be there. Along with them they brought bitterness, envy, strife, and their big brother ANGER! My sister, my friend, we must deal if we want to heal.

Our young hearts cry Daddy! Daddy! Where are you? Oh, how we long to hear the voice of our fathers respond. "Here I am daughter". And as we run into his arms he holds them wide open for his warm embrace. "Why? Why does that even matter to us? Am I not my own person? Can I not function separately from him?"

Some of us know exactly where our fathers are, and some of us do not. Many may know his name, what state he resides in and even what he looks like. Many may not. I have heard many tragic stories of women who were abused, molested or even worse raped by their own fathers! In other situations, women know their fathers first name but have never seen his face. Others lost their fathers in tragedy and have nothing but a memory. While we may all have different beginnings, we share the same ending. We have become Fatherless daughters. The pain that runs through you and I is almost unexplainable at times. I want to pick up the phone and ask my father to "fix it", but I cannot. I want him to help me choose the right mate, or remind me that I'm still his beautiful little girl and ultimately I just want to know I am loved and I want to know WHO I AM! I can handle the rest! Who will validate me, accept me, and love me when the world turns its back to me? These and a plethora of other questions run through our minds in the course of a day.

We have ended up in horrible relationships because of this feeling. Our longing for love led us to the arms of anybody who would say "I love you". Love became a balled up fist and we called it "protection". We just wanted to be "the apple of his eye". We just wanted to feel wanted. We just wanted to feel 'special". We have chosen bad mates because we were looking for a replacement for somebody that could not be replaced. If we watched an abusive father, we may have dated an abuser. The search for "Mr. Right?" I am sorry to inform you, is never ending. Your void you are attempting to fill is not just any man, it's your daddy.

Again, since MY daddy is NOT here, and I have tolerated his absence this long, why are we talking about this again? I know these are the thoughts of many. Trust me, I have heard the stories. Sister, please be attentive to   your inner cries for help. Put aside the long to do list. You are important enough to stop what you are doing and take care of YOU. We as women are so strong that we carry everything but seldom decide to put anything down long enough to deal with ourselves. Many of us have been carrying the bag of fatherlessness for well over 20 years. I pray that since you have the book in your hand, you will decide this is the last year you will carry pain in your heart. This is the last time you will enter into a relationship you can clearly see is not going to work, just to have someone hold you at night. This is the last time you will walk around unloved and unlovable because you allow your pain to shield you and your fears to fight for you. Are you ready to deal with the hand you were dealt? I am.

Daddy Please Don't Go

Nestled under my covers I felt him shake me to awaken me from my sleep. Yawning, "Goodbye daddy", I whispered in my father's ear as he leaned over my bed to kiss me before he left for the day. "Remember it's not goodbye," he replied. "I will see you later baby girl". He was preparing to leave for work early Saturday morning as he always had. "Are you coming to have your car washed today? We are raising money to go to Carowinds with the youth of the church", I said. "I sure am as I wouldn't miss it for the world." "You promise?" I replied. He leaned in for one last hug and said, "Have I ever let you down? I promise", he responded with surety. He then left for work like any other day.

If you would have asked me if my father could do any wrong, my answer would have been no. He was the perfect daddy in my eyes. He always came through for me. He always protected me. He always showed us how much he loved us. He taught me love and sacrifice. He even raised my sister who is not his biological child and never treated her differently. That's true love! He was the first example of unconditional love I had ever known. No matter what we needed, he was always right there.

I never saw him fight, but he must have been great, because he was a U. S. Army soldier! He got suited up every day to fight for our country, and our family. I never feared that I would be in trouble because all I had to do was call my daddy. Even when I was being disciplined I knew it was only because my mother was making him do it. At least that's what he would tell me anyway. My daddy was my number one cheerleader. He always told me to go for it! It didn't matter what it was, he wanted to see me succeed. He was my ace in the hole.

As a young child I was always in competition or performing somewhere. When I would look out into the crowd he would be right there, standing in his uniform being the proud father and soldier. He always kept his promise to return, even if it was at the last minute. One memory I have is when he left to go to Korea. He had to leave for one year! That was a long time in my eyes. My little heart was broken but he promised he would come back, and he did.

His promises to me never came back invalid, until that day. Little did I know those tender words spoken by my father would be his last words to me. Later never came. The same words that once gave me life on a daily basis would be the same words that would leave me abandoned, rejected, bitter, heartbroken, torn and scarred for life.

As told to me, my mother received the call from the hospital later that day. With a low, calm voice the nurse spoke sweetly to my mother, "gather your family and come to the hospital, Roosevelt has been in an accident and he is not responding". My mother contacted me at the fundraiser and told me to be ready when she got there. Questions rang out and tears began to roll down our cheeks. My mom said she tried to ask the nurse what happened, but regrettably all she would say was "I cannot discuss the details over the phone with you. Please come to the hospital now". So, we ventured on, to face our uncertain future. Silence evaded the space in the car as we traveled down the road. Nobody could form their mouths to say much of anything. The silent unspoken prayer was, "God let him be okay." Suddenly, a thirty minute ride, felt like three dreadful hours.

15

We arrived at the hospital and were quickly led to the family room where we were welcomed by hospital staff and our other family members. Standing amongst the crowd at the hospital where we had been called to appear were my father's parents, brothers, sisters, children, nieces and nephews. Maintaining hope in this situation, my first question was "When can we go in and see him"? My mother asked the staff, "Any updates on his condition?" Shortly after we asked these questions, we received the worst possible answer. The nurse, put her head down and placed her hand on my mom's shoulder and spoke the outcome we had feared the most: "Roosevelt Hunt is no longer with us." NOOOOO!! Cries began to permeate throughout the family room. "Please! Tell me it's not true", my mom screamed. My heart was racing so fast at the words she had just spoken. I hear what you are saying, but I do not believe you. I thought to myself, no longer with us. No longer with us! What? What happened? Why are we here? Who did this? Let me see my daddy! The nurse looked down at my tear filled face and said, "I'm sorry. Your father has passed away". Dead? My father is dead? My father was healthy, he was ex-military. He's a natural born survivor! His worst bad habit was smoking cigarettes. Somebody, Please Answer me! He told me he would see me later! He wouldn't lie to me.

He told me I was his baby girl. Please God! Don't do this to me! I asked around until somebody answered the most difficult question of all. How did he die? Suicide? NO…He wouldn't have taken his own life. Not my daddy. He was in the military. He had fought wars and didn't die! My daddy would not do this. He loved us too much. He told me this morning it's not goodbye! He said I will see you later! You promised Daddy! Discouraging thoughts began to flood my mind as tears rolled down my face.

Was I not worth living for? Why would you do this to me? Did my mom not love you enough? Did I not love you enough? Thus, began the journey that would thread these unanswered questions throughout my life for the next 20 years.

I will see you later. My father never came back. However, guess who did show up to take his place? Emptiness, abandonment, rejection, confusion, anger and disappointment are the words that best described my new "friends". I welcomed them with open arms. They promised to always be there for me. Though, I am being sarcastic, but I am also being real.

This was unfair. I was raised in church all my life. I was a good kid. I made good grades and stayed out of trouble. This wasn't supposed to happen to me. What had I done to my father to make him want to leave me here all alone? What had we done to God to make him take my father away? I had so many questions and no one had the answers. "The Lord giveth and the Lord taketh away" doesn't really answer the questions of a broken hearted 12 year old girl.

The days ahead were extremely difficult. To add insult to injury 7 months later, my grandmother, his mother, was called home to be with God as well. Another person that I loved dearly had been taken from me. More feelings of abandonment set in. At 12 years old, I could not have relayed to you what the full definition of abandonment was, but I sure knew what it felt like. I felt horrible. I wasn't just dealing with death. I had dealt with death before. I was dealing with something that was a lot bigger than me. I was feeling too weak to fight it and it was winning.

Looking back on that day I wish I would had someone to tell me - YOU ARE LOVED. You are the daughter of the King. Period. Point blank. No questions. So I say this to you, you are loved daughter. Daughter, your father is near and will save you from your broken heart.

> **The Lord is near to those who have a broken heart, and saves such as have a contrite spirit. Psalm 34:18**

Be it mother, father, sister, brother, friend, the quality of your existence is not tied to another human being. Even if that human being helped bring you into this world, what we must deal with is maintaining our identity in the face of loss and conflict. As a child, I was just beginning to learn who I was when my world fell apart.

As daughters we are introduced to our fathers as our first male/female relationship. My daddy was my first boyfriend! Most girls when they are little say "I am going to marry my daddy". That is merely a foreshadowing of things to come; what we really mean is we want to marry the kind of man our fathers are to us, it's in our nature. We want to marry 3 things: a provider, a protector and a leader.

Men were originally designed to keep order in the family. The opposite of order is chaos. So if you lack having a relationship with a person of order, then ultimately, something in your life is in chaos. The relationship, or lack thereof, with our fathers helps mold and shape our reality. My 12 year old reality was death. Now, your reality may be a past reality but if it still hurts, then it is probably still real to you, and you must deal with the issues that have scarred your heart.

My father was dead and so was I. Not literally as I had wished but I was just as cold, empty and lifeless. Sounds like a dead body to me.

As I stood by his graveside, I watched as my identity was lowered into the ground. Help me. I feel like I am losing breath with every day that passes. I feel as if I am suffocating. "God where are you now?" I cried silently. I wished I had been buried with him. I didn't know who I was, what I was going to do, what I should do next, and the worst part was that I didn't have anyone to confide in. Everyone else seemed to go on with their lives and suggested I do the same. So I existed in silent frustration. I harbored all kinds of anger inside of me. I was mad at the world. Mostly, I was mad at God.

After my father passed away, I was considerably mouthy, attitudinal, angry and rebellious. I probably, no I am sure; I gave my mother a headache daily. The pain I felt inside became so unbearable that I let everybody on the outside have a piece of my pain. It was like emotional vomit. I refused to hold my tongue for any reason. It was coming out whenever, however or wherever! Nobody could say or tell me anything. I had found a new excuse, and I liked it, "You are not my daddy". I was going to do whatever I was big and bad enough to do. My attitude was mine and nobody could take that away from me. In some twisted way, I felt as if it offered me some control over others and it didn't matter if it was male or female. The world had been evil to me, and I was going to be evil right back. There was nothing anyone could do or say to bring him back, and no one would ever again be worthy of my respect.

Even as I got older, up to my late teens, this attitude stuck with me a long time. I remember boldly declaring this to my uncle for the last and final time. I had purchased a shiny black 89' Trans-Am with T-tops from him. She was so sweet! I parked it in the middle of my front yard, filled the bucket with water and went back in the house. As I pranced my happy self back out of the house the second time I had on a bikini! Yep! I was having my very own bikini car wash in my own front yard! My uncle was LIVID! He showed how much by demanding that I go in the house. "Why! "You are not my daddy and I refuse to listen to what you tell me what to do," I screamed and added a slight head roll for affect.

You have to understand that my uncle just right next door, so he was always there. I mean literally. We could not get away with ANYTHING without him seeing it and demanding it be changed. He was just being an uncle and looking back I am thankful. He saved me when I was not even trying to save myself. Needless to say, I washed my car in basketball shorts and a t-shirt that day. "I may not be your daddy, but unless you want to join him, go put some clothes on". "Yes sir", I responded as I quickly ran in the house to avoid any more trouble. From that day on, I didn't use that line anymore. He really was looking out for my best interests. However, at that time he was just another man, who tried to be in authority over me. I had decided at the grown up age of 13, there would never be another man in authority over me. The man that was supposed to hold that position was gone.

These were the thoughts that pierced my mind and they were constant and consistent. I was rude to everybody I came in contact with, and nobody could really understand why. As the years went by I guess they expected me to "get over it" but the pain just got worse, and the wounds got deeper. My uncles and grandfather were there to help my mother when she needed a male influence but there was nothing like having your own father. I wanted MY father back! Sadly, there was nothing I, or anybody else, could do to bring him back. Would this pain ever go away?

The much anticipated "high school days" had arrived and I entered the 9th grade with great expectation. My dad had always told us excelling in academics was one of the most important achievements in this lifetime. I wanted so badly to make him proud of me as I walked into the new school equipped and ready to learn. A few of my friends were aware of what happened to my father over the summer, but not many, so I was able to put on a happy face for the most part. Unfortunately, I was not ready for what High School had to offer.

I entered high school with my middle school mentality. In middle school, I rarely studied. Subjects were easy for me to comprehend and I still made the honor roll. "If it ain't broke, don't fix it" right? WRONG! The classes seemed to be somewhat challenging at first. This was nothing like Middle School had been! Classes were too long, and break wasn't long enough. I had a hard time adjusting to high school. Focusing in those hour and half long classes only made me narcoleptic and I would often fall asleep. I think I was still paralyzed by the death of my father and the only thing that brought me relief was to sleep my pain away. The worst part was that my teachers would rarely wake me up! One teacher boldly informed me, "If that's what you want to do with your life, do it". So I agreed with a silent head nod, went back to sleep.

I really didn't know at the time, I was using sleep as a form of comforting myself in the place where I hurt the most. I was clinically depressed. I struggled with everything but English. That seemed to come easily to me. The biggest challenge I faced was studying. I didn't study in middle school and I made A's and B's, so I thought I could do the same in high school. Boy was I wrong! The first nine weeks report card was issued and I was completely devastated. I knew I had not done well, but this was beyond bad!

21

This was horrible! I would have to show my mother that I was making D's and F's.

Immediately this thought came to mind: I AM A FAILURE. This is the identity I gave myself, as I already knew that was what everyone was going to think of me. I had been too afraid to ask for help, so I pretended I knew everything, when I indeed knew nothing.

After the first report card came out, my teacher was concerned because my grade history coming from middle school had been A's and B's. They were all very concerned. My teacher asked if something was wrong at home. I told her nothing was wrong and I promised to do better. She called my mom anyway to schedule a conference with all my teachers and the guidance counselor. I couldn't help thinking, "Wow, an intervention on my behalf? It's really not that serious. Lord, how did I let this happen?" Out of my 10 years of being in school, I NEVER had to have a parent/teacher conference about bad grades. Can you imagine the ride on the way to school? It was almost as bad as the ride to the hospital. I knew she wasn't going to kill me, but I couldn't promise she wasn't going to try! Dead silence filled the air. My mom said nothing, just glancing at me every few minutes as if she wanted to slap me. I was so scared.

Once we arrived at the school the question was repeatedly asked, what happened? So I was forced to face the facts again, the hardcore truth. Facts I thought I had put behind me. My mom waited for me to answer, but I just put my head down. She answered the teacher's question. Brandy's father died over the summer. "Ms. Hunt, I'm so sorry to hear that", the teacher replied. "Now I understand". She continued to state that this type of behavior often occurs when children have experienced the death of a parent or a close loved one. My mother said that was no excuse and I was raised better than that. And she was right, I was, but this pain was winning and I am unable to determine what to next. My teachers said they would do their best to help me get through it. Or get over it. That's all people want you to ever do is get over it.

My mom smiled in all the conferences and didn't slap me like I know she wanted. But MAMA let me have it when we got back to the house. It was fair though. The unnecessary attitude I had given her over the past few months, I deserved all she did and more.

After she cooled off, my mom made an agreement with me that if my grades improved to A's and B's, I could try out for the Varsity cheerleading team. Since I was a little girl I had wanted to be a cheerleader. In my eyes, cheerleaders were pretty, athletic, motivational and loved by ALL! These were all important factors to me because I was unloved, no pretty, unimportant, and unmotivated! I could not identify where these feelings of insecurity came from but all of a sudden I had this feeling of wanting to be recognized. I felt unimportant. I wanted people to accept me for who I was. I never felt that before my father died. I felt as if it was his fault because I was now required to deal with all these emotions.

After much hard work, and a full 9 weeks of punishment, I got A's, B's, and 1 C on the next report card. I felt better, even accomplished. I got my mom off my back, but something was still missing. Not quite sure what it was I ventured on to see what life had to offer. Mom let the "C" slide because she knew I had tried really hard! Off to cheerleading tryouts I went. Yay me!

The day of tryouts I was a nervous wreck. At this point, I had never auditioned for anything before. This was a big step for me because I knew it meant facing the judges. Judges meant judgment and rejection if I didn't make it. Despite the fear and anxiety I felt, I knew I was talented and confident to land my spot on the cheerleading squad. That's one thing my daddy taught me well. Anybody that knew him would say "your daddy thinks he is all that". Because he thought he was, he was! He also taught me "even in the midst of adversity, we "Hunts" do it with a smile.

I remember when he and my mother would argue he would find something to smile about. He would often turn his face and wink at me and grin. I think that was to help me see that he really loved my mother and that argument wasn't going to last long. I opened the gymnasium doors I picked my head up and I walked into tryouts nervous, afraid, sad and excited all at the same time. Daddy I hope I make you proud, my heart fluttered.

"Brandy Hunt, welcome to the team!" I remember hearing my name called and it felt like they were announcing the winner of the Miss America pageant. Tears filled my face. They probably thought it was because I really wanted to be a cheerleader. The real truth was that I felt alive again. That dark cloud that seemed to hover over me was gone. My life lit up like a child's face on Christmas morning! That emptiness I once felt so deep was now fulfilled. I felt as if I actually mattered in this world. Somebody sees me. I'm not invisible.

Making the cheerleading team just wasn't about using my talents. I knew I was talented. I wanted to know that I was accepted in this world and that I could make a difference. I looked different, I acted differently, and I even talked different. More importantly, I was ok with my uniqueness. I just really needed to know that I was beautiful in someone else's eyes. I wanted to hear those words again "hey beautiful". The moment I heard my name called was unforgettable. The horrible, gut wrenching pain that had stalked me for two years finally went away and was replaced with laughter, confidence and the surety that I could move on with my life. I knew in my heart I had made my daddy proud.

During this transitional period of my life, the thoughts that manifested through my mind will and emotions at times felt unbearable. Asking me "how did I get here?" would not have been the proper question. The only answer at that time I had was: be alive. All I had done up until this point was live. I was handed fatherlessness as a card I would have to deal with for the rest of my life. I repeatedly reminded myself I didn't do anything to lose my father, things happen. Life happens. I kept questioning myself. Why had the death of my father created such a loss inside of me that I needed some type of accomplishment to tell me that I was still important? That I was still righteous? That I was still the daughter of the King even though my earthly father was gone? I was confused.

When you do not know who you are in Christ it's easy to operate in who you are not. Satan wants to get to us at an early age because we are still vulnerable and easily swayed. When we are young we are very impressionable. Something began to permeate in my spirit that I needed to be affirmed and validated. I needed to be told that I was beautiful. I needed to be told I was still loved and wanted. I had a self-esteem problem that never existed before! My value had diminished. Self-love was now no love. I had a void that needed to be filled, and in my mind the quicker I could fill it the better.

No matter the reason for the passing of a loved one, death is untimely. It's painful and it doesn't have any remorse for the people that it leaves behind to deal with the pain. The void left by abandonment leaves several thoughts sketched on your mind: Why am I not good enough and what did I do to God to make him punish me so? I was helpless and hopeless, stuck in a twirling vortex of Satan's lies.

My Not So Sweet 16

Sweet 16 huh? What's so sweet about it? During my earlier years I had waited in great anticipation for this day to come. It had been about three years since my father had passed away. Life was somewhat back to "normal". My grades were still good. Cheerleading was going well and it was usually the highlight of my day. It was the only time I felt "alive". Home was still really gloomy to me as we still lived in the same house after my father passed away; thus, it was a constant reminder of his absence. Not to mention my mother had remarried. I'm sure you can feel my enthusiasm.

Yes, we had a new daddy! Can you relate? I am sure you can imagine and maybe even relate. That was a tough transition. I wouldn't have wanted to be that guy as he had some pretty big shoes to fill. I understood my mom, being single with 3 kids, wanted to give us the best replacement she could find and still keep her sanity. At this point, we were older now: 11, 15, and 19. We had something to say and unfortunately for him, it was too much. Now that I am older and have gone through similar experiences, I can relate to my mother. Pain makes choices for us that we would not ordinarily make if we were not heartbroken. But just like me, my mother was dealing with the loss of her lover, best friend, and husband. She too was looking for love, to be loved, and to be validated. She was looking for a "normal" that no longer existed.

Nevertheless, I was still excited about turning 16. Since everyone made a big deal about it, I thought something amazing would happen for me too! The people on television always had a huge celebration; sort of like a coming of age party. But for what would I celebrate? My father would never be able to watch me cheer at a football game or tell me how pretty I was when all the kids pick on me. He was not here to tell me about dating, save me from my siblings beating up on me, teach me how to love, teach me how to drive, take me on my first date, or save me from my first rape. Rape? Yes, Rape.

Evening had set in and we were all gathered at my house to watch a few movies and hang out. Among the crew were myself, my sister, my best friend and some of our male companions. My mom had turned in to go to bed for the evening. "Goodnight everyone, I could care less about what you do, just stay in the living room." That was as much as my mom would say regarding knowing how to act like a lady, just keep the boys out of our rooms. And we happily did so. My mother allowed us room to have fun, but advised us to stay out of trouble. And we always did so. My sister is 4 years older than me, so I always felt comfortable with her around. Nobody could beat her! At least not from what I had witnessed. She was my personal body guard. I knew no one would mess with me if she was somewhere close by. Mom bid us goodnight and went to sleep. Once we heard her snoring we knew she was out for good until the next morning.

At 16, I was the youngest among the crowd and apparently the most naïve. "Here, taste this" I was politely commanded by my male companion, as he handed me a red cup. "What is it?" I asked. "Here just drink it - it's sweet. You will like it", he said. I sipped slowly in disbelief. "Oh! It IS sweet", I replied with a foolish grin. "What is it?" I naively giggled. "It's a mixed drink. It won't do you any harm," his friend chimed in to help convince me. A few drunken minutes later I would find out this "mixed drink" would be the catalyst used to change my life forever. The evening faded quickly along with my vision and my spunk. "I'm hungry", my sister said. "Let's go eat." "Yes! Let's do so," I slurred. As I stood up, I quickly tumbled back down to the couch. "Brandy, you are unable to go out like this. We will bring you back something to eat. And he will stay here with you", pointing at his male companion. "No! Don't leave me here with him", I begged.

Prior to this evening he had suggested that we have sex and attempted to do so several times. I told him what I told everybody else, no as I was waiting until I got married. We could be friends but that was it. He thought that was stupid and said that people didn't do that anymore. I didn't realize that he was determined to make a believer out of me.

"Girl, you're stumbling, not walking", my sister blurted out sarcastically. "You cannot go out in public with me. You will go to jail for public drunkenness AND underage drinking. Not on my watch. It's 3:00am. Just go to bed, we will be back in about an hour", she convincingly replied. "Fine, wake me up when you get back. I'm going to bed", I said.

Staggering down the hall, my companion followed closely behind me to make sure I got to bed safely, so he said. I quickly turned around and slurred, "I'm fine, now go back to the living room. You heard my momma say, nobody can come back here, especially boys!" I attempted to push him away but he caught me mid fall. He then guided me to the bedroom. "Get out of here. You're going to get me in trouble", I said sternly. His CROOKED response was, "Your mom is asleep, and she will never hear us". My heart raced. I should have screamed and ran as my mom was only doors away. Fear set in and silence took over.

As he began to swiftly remove my shirt he asked, "Do you want to change clothes"? "No", I quickly replied and dropped my arms down. My heart began to race faster. "Just go back in the living room. You are not allowed to be back here! You heard what my mom said". "She's asleep. Just be quiet. She won't hear us. You said you wanted to be my girl right?" "Well, yeah, but not like this. I also said I wanted to be married, but I don't see a ring", I said sarcastically. I crawled into a ball, for I knew my fate and it was not good. As he turned the lights out I prayed, Oh God, please help me. A little voice in my head said run now, so I tried.

He pushed me back down on the bed. I tried to apply what force I could find to fight him off of me, but the mixed drink concoction was preventing me from doing so. Also, he was a 6' tall linebacker and I was only 130lbs, 5' tall and drunk. "No! Stop! ," I squealed. "Why are you doing this? I told you I didn't want to have sex until I got married! Ouch! You're hurting me!" "Be quiet! I know what women want!   Be still and it won't hurt." He covered my mouth, but it really wasn't necessary. For fear that my mom would awaken, I had already stopped yelling. I lay there crying in silence thinking, Daddy please come save me. Of course, my daddy never came.

My sister returned to find me curled in the fetal position in my bed, crying, awake, but unresponsive, and scarred. "Brandy, what's wrong?" I wouldn't answer. I just lie there with a blank stare. She began to question him and search for answers. After frantically rushing to and fro from my bedroom to hers she found the undeniable evidence. He had taken the bloody sheets that had been removed from her bed and stuffed them in a closet, now she had her answer. "I'm sorry", she said in a whisper. "I'm so sorry. I shouldn't have left you here." "It's not your fault," I said. "Do not put so much blame yourself. It's my fault," I whimpered. I never told my mother, and I went on with my life.

Again, my innocence was stolen from me. I didn't ask for this to happen. Another card has been dealt to me and I do not have a clue what to do about it. For a second time my identity was buried under the lies of fear, loneliness, rejection, abandonment, abuse and anger.

Almost 3 years had gone by since my father passed away. I had "gotten over it" as I was told to do so many times about my father's passing. Obviously, I never really got over it. I just found other ways to be happy and enjoy the rest of my existence without him. The fact still remained that I didn't know what to do with my life without him in it and I really didn't even understand why life mattered anymore. I remember asking myself "was I destined to be a victim of circumstance all my life?" Why were people just allowed to take things from me that didn't belong to them? I thought I had done everything "right." I was raised in church, purity WAS my goal. I promised God and myself I would wait to have sex until I was married. I even preached it to all my friends!

By the age of 16 most girls I knew had already tried out kissing, gone on their first date, or went "all the way" and had sex. But I was going to be different. I was picked on by my friends for not having done it already. I was okay with that. I was taught by the church folks that I should wait for my husband. Those are the girls that get respect. Those are the women who have the "good life". Christian women are supposed to have higher standards. So, I set out on a journey of purity to only be faced with adversity? I don't get it. This man, thought it best to leave me scarred for the rest of my life. His instant gratification would eventually lead to my long term suffering.

The feelings I endured after this tragic incident were almost unexplainable. I was a beautiful mansion on the outside, but dirt and rubble on the inside. Now I am fatherless, no longer "pure" and a victim of rape. Am I even still a Christian? Can somebody tell me who am I now? Apparently this purity thing is NOT what Christian women do, if it was then God would have shielded me from what happened. So, I had a new discovery and goal. My newest discovery: sex. My newest goal: find a man that really loves me. What was sex really supposed to be like? Since I have already ruined my "little miss perfect" image, and won't be able to stay a virgin until I got married, I might as well find out what it was really supposed to be like. Since I am no longer "pure" what am I? FILTHY? Since I am empty who should fill me up again? I am broken, who should fix me? Since I am no longer valuable, I will need to find somebody who will value me.

So this is where I began my journey to find "true love" and the "real" me. In my opinion, if the old me had been any good, he would not have treated me the way he did and God would not have allowed it.

Dear Daughter,

Come to me you, and I will give you rest. I love you daughter. I fashioned you to be a mighty woman of God from the foundations of the world. I knew you even before you knew yourself. Before I introduced you to the world I formed you in your mother's womb. I can't tell you how it breaks my heart to see you crying. I don't want to see you in pain or be discouraged. The trials of this life are many, but I will deliver you from them all. Hold on to me. I have a wonderful plan for your life. I love to hear you sing to me. I love to see you dance. I am enthralled by your beauty. I am proud of you. You are not beautiful, full of beauty. You ARE beauty. When I thought of how to define beauty, I created you. You are far more precious than rubies, better than fine gold. You were so amazing that I created you as an answer to prayer! You are necessary to the forward movement of those around you.. I chose you from the foundation of the world for such a time as this. You are destined to be a world changer. Do not be afraid to go into the unknown and unfamiliar territories, I am with you. I have given you power and authority to conquer the enemy. You are safe.

Purest Love,

Your Father

The Fatherless Daughter

Fatherless daughter? Though it sounds a bit twisted and backwards, I felt like I was backwards, so that described me perfectly. I was born into this world to Roosevelt and Sandra Hunt. I expected it to be this way for my entire life. I was accustomed to having a father and mother; though now I only had my mother. When I started this Christian journey I was pure. I made sure that I did not have sex before I was married so that God and my family would still love me. But I was raped, I was defiled. My purity was compromised, so what now? No one is going to want me. Does God still want me? Does that make me a tainted Christian? This was just not fair! I tried so hard to ignore the evil suggestions that flooded my mind telling me how nasty and filthy I was for what I had done. But when the external voices and the internal voices started to match, I had no choice but to believe them. I did not know at the time that my circumstances had no right to change my name. Whomever God called me from the foundations of this earth is who I am; regardless of the hand I was dealt. Unfortunately, I did not know my identity and my fearful lifeless journey continued.

I thought to myself, life is just not fair. Well that is one true statement. You do not get to pick the cards you are dealt. Everybody does not get the same hand.

The next card I was dealt after abandonment was emptiness. I felt dead inside all over again. I think this time was worse. It was like I was an empty container. The container still exists, but there is nothing inside. Emptiness is not one of those feelings that you can just shake off whenever you get ready.

Empty is defined as containing nothing; having none of the usual or appropriate contents. (dictionary.com)

Yep, that describes me alright. My heart felt cold and numb. I could not even force a smile. I began to not only feel empty but also, angry.

The only time empty can change its identity is to fill it with something. Regardless of what you fill it with, it is no longer empty it is either full, almost full, half full, etc. but it is not empty. The situations and circumstances had drained the life out of me to the point that I was empty. I had cried all my tears out and yelled at the sky until I couldn't speak anymore. I had nothing inside of me to give away anymore. This is what is called emotional emptiness.

Emotional Emptiness is defined as lack of meaning or purpose. When you experience loss and are left empty, the enemy will come quickly with suggestions on what we should fill it with. Your emptiness is the result of a deep desire to reconnect with something or someone you love. But what if the thing you love is no longer available to connect to? How does a 13 year old recover from losing her father and even worse, her own identity? I thought losing my father was the worst thing I could have gone through, until I lost me. My father wasn't lost. God knew exactly where his soul was resting. I was still among the living, yet I wanted to die. I wanted anything that would make the pain go away. At this point I think I had tried mostly everything to relieve myself of emptiness, but nothing worked. I even tried joining in more activities at church to keep my mind occupied. I tried anything that kept me saved, safe and out of trouble. Ultimately, nothing helped.

Tragedy and trauma can come in all forms. Mine was losing my father, for some, it may have been your mother, or even your child. Tragedy and Trauma (TNT) are the TNT of the emotional world. Trinitrotoluene, better known as TNT is an explosive. It is used when something needs to be blown up. What makes it explosive is that it is chemically unstable. The exact same thing occurs in the human mind. A person that is emotionally unstable will blow up and spill out over everything. They have TNT in their minds. Just like TNT blows up things into an unrecognizable state so does our mind. Any mixture of emotions such as rage, anger, loneliness, bitterness, abandonment, self-hatred, low self-esteem and even suicidal thoughts can cause a person to blow! If these emotions go untreated you can expect your next blow up to occur at any moment now! What blows us up inside will typically come out in our mouths and our actions.

I am sure you have heard doctors and counselors say certain mental illnesses are caused by a chemical imbalance in the brain or hormonal system. You are a walking time bomb and just like TNT can blow up, so can you! The world refers to this with descriptions such as, "melt down", "nervous breakdown" or "fits of anger". When you hear they just "snapped". That is not true. They didn't just get upset that day. They have been sitting on their stock NT for a while now, and by not dealing with the issue that was causing the imbalance, they blew up. Furthermore, when TNT blows up, depending on the amount of chemicals that were inside, it can damage everything around it for miles. It is the same with people. When you blow up, or break down, you will damage more than just yourself, you will damage everything and everybody around. DEAL WITH IT, BEFORE IT DEALS WITH YOU!

As a fatherless daughter who has not dealt with the pain of the past, a range of emotions can flood you at any point of the day. Like an unexpected flashflood pain will come through and wash away what little bit of happiness you may have had at that moment. Let me make you are aware right now; the enemy of our mind is a deceiver. He will flood your mind with billions of lies and negative thoughts at one time. He does not care if you drown! He only comes to steal, kill and destroy.

I did not know at the time that I was not "dealing" with what I was going through, that I was just going through the motions. E-motions. E for empty-motions. Nothingness. I would feel certain emotions at times, but I didn't know how to properly handle them. I continued to ignore them, laugh them off or pretend like they were not there. Those were defense mechanisms; sort of like a shield. Anytime someone would get close to me I would just smile and say "I'm ok". That is not dealing, that is coping, better yet, hiding. I felt as if I was handling it the best way I could, so I considered it done. At this pace I was headed for a major blow up and I didn't even know it.

Cheerleading Practice 1997

"Ready! Ok! We are the Tigers oh yeah, (stomp clap) and we're here to compete (stomp clap), we're so fine, the Tiger fans are jumping out of their seat", the cheerleaders screamed in unison. We jumped and shouted as if we had already won the game. However, we were just in practice. Now, in case you are not a cheerleading expert, just so you know, we were trained that each cheer ends with some type of victory jump. My favorite, considering I had become great at it, was a toe touch. I had done this jump at least a hundred times. Each time it got better. Let's go tigers! I jumped up to complete my jump and.... crunch! "AAAAAAHHHHH! God!" I wailed. "Brandy, are you ok?" my coach asked. "No! Call the EMS! Please!", as tears began to roll down my face as the pain of a busted knee began to surface. Somebody get some ice! "Ice? Did you hear me say my knee cap just twisted out of my leg? Call 911", I whimpered. "Cheerleaders are unable to be insured through the athletic programs at the school, I'm sorry we are not authorized to bring you an ambulance here", my coach replied sympathetically. "You will have to be driven to the hospital." Right before my very eyes my life went from bad to worse. Again, more trauma and tragedy crept upon me and there wasn't a thing I could do about it but live through it. It seemed as if I could not get over one emotional tragedy before I was dealing with the next traumatic experience. I could not handle another one.

To add insult to injury, at the exact same time I was on the floor screaming from my painful fall a wrestler was across the gym and twisted his knee as well. I watched as the emergency personnel rushed in to pick him up and drive him to the hospital. "How come he can get help, but I have to suffer," I screamed. I was informed athletes have school insurance, cheerleaders are not considered athletes. I knew at that moment, life was not fair.

Angry and afraid, I had a friend drive me home instead of the hospital, even though my knee was the size of a grapefruit. I needed to get to my momma. I was in the most excruciating pain I had ever felt in my lifetime. I didn't even go to the doctor the same day. I took some pain medicine and went to sleep. I was secretly praying that it was just swollen and I would be ok. I woke up to my knee being more swollen than the day before and an awful pain that medicine could not get rid of. I got ready to face what I knew was the inevitable as my mother and I went to the hospital.

I hate hospitals. I heard of my fathers' death in a hospital. Hospitals meant bad news so I wasn't surprised at what came next. After many painful x-rays and talking with the doctor he came with this awful response. "Ms. Hunt, you will need to have surgery tomorrow and you will be on crutches for at least 8 weeks." "Tomorrow! But Doctor! Isn't there something else you can do?" "No," he kindly replied. "This kind of injury requires surgery and takes time to heal. It may get worse if you wait any longer." Looking down at his chart, "It shows here that you injured yourself while cheerleading, is that correct"? "Yes," I replied with my head down. "I'm sorry Ms. Hunt; you will not be able to cheer for the rest of the season. Not so bad? There is always next year right?" It would have been except this was my senior year, mid basketball season! So this meant the end for me. I would miss the upcoming cheerleading competition too.

Tears rolled down my face as the only thing that gave me joy, was now bringing me pain. Is that all you doctors know how to say to people? "I'm sorry Ms. Hunt?" Sorry? No you are not! I screamed in my head. First my father dies, and then some creep rapes me, now this? The pain and agony of my internal emotions began to surface on my face in the form of tears and anger found a seat in my heart. Cheerleading was the only thing that gave me life. It was my identity. People liked me and it made me feel special. I would like to say the reason I joined was for the sole reason that it gave me fulfillment and purpose, but that would be a lie.

Cheerleaders wore the cutest outfits, hang with all the athletes and looked good while we did it.

Yes, of course I was good at being a cheerleader. However, as I got older I was becoming even better at being a flirt. NO, It wasn't about having sex with the players! That would have given me a title I couldn't handle. However, they gave me the attention I was lacking. Standing up in front of crowds of people and being important was filling my void. Now what? High school was soon to be over in less than 8 months, so I should just go on with my life and prepare for my future right? Let's look at what I had planned for my future:

Fatherless daughters tend to not have a lot of order in their lives, nor good strategies. They are like arrows just shot up in the sky to land anywhere. My mother had two requests of me: graduate from high school and do it without having a baby. Cool, I didn't want kids anyway and I always planned to complete high school. I would have NEVER considered being a high school dropout. So mom, we have a deal! My after high school plan, that's another story. I was conflicted. Plan A would be the United States Army, unless of course I become part of the Dallas Cowgirls! Plan B? SC State University on a cheerleading scholarship until I become a Dallas Cowgirl. Of course I wasn't going to only cheer; I was going to study Psychology. I had beauty and brains.

I knew that going to the Army would make my daddy proud but my mother was terrified. At the point of my injury I had already weighed in and taken the entry test for the Army. I passed all the necessary requirements. My friends tried to talk me out of it. However, I was determined to follow in my daddy's footsteps and become a United States Army Soldier. My mom didn't want me to go, but she said if that's what would make me happy then she would support me. Unfortunately my next let down was my recruiter informing me that due to having knee surgery the U.S. Army required me to wait for 1-2 years and be re-evaluated. I would need to retest and basically start from scratch. Major upset! More rejection!

Doors were constantly being closed in my face. I could not audition for the cheerleading team at SC University for the scholarship because I was still on crutches. I thought I was intelligent but definitely not smart enough to get an academic scholarship, at least that's what I believed anyway. I had A's, B's and a few C's at best, my GPA was maybe a 2.75, but what did that matter now? My dreams were shattered. I hobbled myself through my last year of high school without a solid plan for my life and I once again felt like a complete failure. I began to feel depressed, lonely, abandoned and discouraged. I couldn't seem to escape these emotions. Every 2 years I was faced with them! I didn't have another plan. I was so devastated that my plan wasn't working out.

I was trying desperately to look past myself and hear what the preacher said. Yeah. I was still in church. We went on Sundays and Wednesdays, and sometimes Friday. Unfortunately, I couldn't hear the preacher past my own thoughts. In my mind I'm still asking God why? Why me? Is what I have asked for too hard to deliver? Everybody else is getting on with their lives and I'm stuck! None of this was my fault. I had been "perfect". I tried really hard to obtain and maintain high morals and standards so that people would not look at me as less than perfect. I tried to be the "good girl" so I could live the "good life". As I took inventory of my close friends and family I realized everybody was going away to college, except for me. I thought God was mad at me, so he punished me by making me stay in a city I really didn't want to be in.

I knew that if my daddy were here he would have fixed it for me. Fixed what you ask? How about my heart, my will, and my emotions? He would have pushed me to keep going. He would have given me the extra encouragement that I needed from a father. But he left me here by myself! I'm nobody and I'm not going anywhere with my life. These were thoughts and feelings I began to have on a constant and consistent basis.

After I was raped I found myself curious about what sex should really have been like. I eventually found myself drawn to the opposite sex. I wasn't running from them, as I had been. Now I was running to them. The whistles that were once felt as disrespectful and degrading were now welcomed. I was rather shapely and cute, and always got lots of attention from men. I began to feed off of that attention because for some reason it made that feeling of emptiness go away. Even though it was only temporary, it was good to feel wanted. They would say things like "hey beautiful", Do you know what that does to a girl when she feels ugly and unwanted? That one phrase has the ability to change her whole world.

I never thought I was just downright ugly. I never really entertained thoughts of low self-esteem. I may have not thought I was the prettiest girl in the room, but I sure didn't think I was the ugliest either. My father's smile would light up a room, and he left it with me. He thought very highly of himself and taught us to do the same. He told me to never let anybody talk you out of who you know you are. I could hear his voice in my head telling me these things, but even pretty gets lonely. I did have long seasons of feeling unaccepted and unloved. I felt if I went missing nobody would care. My voids ran deep. It was almost as if nothing I could find externally was big enough to fill this void I had inside of me, but I was sure going to keep trying to ease the pain.

Being a fatherless daughter was one of the most painful truths I have had to endure. I was tired of the pain. People find themselves addicted to all kinds of things to ease their pain and troubled minds. Drugs tend to be the answer for physical pain. Be it street drugs or prescription. They ease pain, and if you are not careful you can become addicted and dependent. I knew I would never do drugs though, as it was a catalyst to what caused my fathers' death. What about emotional pain? I needed to find something to help ease the horrible effects of my incurable disease-fatherlessness. So began my journey to ease the pain.

Foolishness.com

Riddle me this: Where can you go to find anything and everything in this world you want at the click of a button? You guessed it! The World Wide Web, www. The internet. No matter what you are looking for; there is somebody on the other end of that click to give you what you are lacking. If you are not strong enough to withstand the temptation of the enemy, any and all manner of evil temptation is waiting at the doors of www.

The internet is the perfect solution to a worldwide epidemic of loneliness in a generation of people with unmet needs. There are millions of people around the world that log into internet chat rooms, Facebook, Twitter, and Instagram on a daily basis just looking for a connection. They will probably disagree with me, but it's true. No, not everybody on social media is lonely, but many lonely people are on social media.

As I stated before, I had big voids inside my heart and mind that seemed to get bigger by the day. The year was somewhere around 1998 and internet chat rooms had just become the newest craze. There was no MySpace, Facebook, Twitter, liking, following, or tweeting as of yet, but what we had to start us off was great too! You mean to tell me I can meet multiple men half way across the world or in my city? I can have conversations about whatever suits my fancy and never leave my living room? I can pick what I like? Tall, short, dark, light, fat, tall, professional, blue collar, white collar, Christian, or no religion at all, kids, no kids, and the list goes on! This is like Baskin-Robins! Sweet! Sign me up! And that's how it all begins.

In answering many of the questions on the profile creator, about yourself and who you are looking for, you get a false sense of choice. You are encouraged to believe that you are actually participating in the choosing process. It's designed to make you feel as if you are in control. At 18 I didn't know what I wanted or who I needed in my life. I barely knew who I was at the time, but hey it's worth a try. It's just a computer right? What I have yet to learn, I can lie about. I mean it's not like they are going to know the truth right?

It wasn't long before I had my first hits and responses from men wanting to "chat". "Chatting" is nothing but talking and talking is harmless right? You know that new feeling you feel when you meet a new friend? I was getting that several times a day! This has to be what drug addiction feels like! I could just log on and get my "fix" and I would INSTANTLY feel better. Yes it's harmless at first, until talking leads to wanting to meet up with you. Let's be clear; not everybody just wants to chat online!

This can be a VERY dangerous environment, but that was okay; I liked living on the edge. It excited me. I was always the daring one of the group. So this venture would be no different. I was still on my search to fill the void. That huge empty gnawing that resided on the inside of me. I didn't know what the empty space was, but I knew exactly what filled it; any combination of validation, confirmation or the attention of men. I didn't even really understand why, but at this point I didn't care. I wasn't a smoker or drinker, so my high was being in the chat room. I felt it to be pretty harmless. It was harmless to my physical body, but my soul was torn into little tiny pieces.

I was ultimately trying to replace the love I lost with new love. However, this love was irreplaceable. I was never ever going to find even a suitable replacement. Even now, as I look back over my life, all the qualities I have ever wanted in a man matched that of my father. In my search all I ever wanted was to be loved. I wanted somebody to pursue, protect and provide for me. I could handle the rest. Oh yeah, and promise not to ever leave me.

You would think after searching hundreds and hundreds of profiles and going on more blind dates than you can count on two hands that I would have found the "one". I didn't want much: a family man, Christian, dedicated, diligent, and valiant. That didn't seem too hard to me. What I did find was ignorance, liars, cheaters, manipulators, and I am sure you get the picture by now. I was even so bold as to actually meet up with some of the guys I met!

He was perfect! At least online anyway. His description said *Average height, Average build, god-fearing, family man, looking for his Queen.* By the way, they all say that. Anyway, we talked a while online, talking about the preliminaries: kids, jobs, career path, and church. We agreed to meet at the local mall, so far so good. If he was going to kill me, he wouldn't meet me at the mall right? I ventured out to meet my new prospect at the local mall. As I walked upon him, he WAS perfect! He stood about 6"0 tall, sweet chocolate brown skin, with those bedroom brown eyes. We walked around and then got something to eat. As time was winding down he was going to work at asked if I would like to come with him. He worked in a lobby of a high rise apartment building, so company in the lobby was fine. Ok, I thought, I am in my own car, so if anything happens I can leave. So we continued our night of hanging out. As the night grew dim, I got tired and suggested that I leave. "Oh, no need, they give me a free room when I get tired. You can go up there and lie down." I hesitated, but then, I agreed. About 20 minutes later he came in and that's when fear set in. He climbed in the bed with me. I was terrified. I didn't want to scream, because I didn't know if he was just expecting to have sex with me all along. I had been pretty "easy" up until this point. I mean, I am a pretty girl, in what is almost like a hotel room, at 1:00am. What else would I be here for? He slid his hand down my body. I began to shake. Fear gripped my mind, body, and mouth. I was silent. Every thought about the first rape flooded my mind, and tears flood my face. No. I whispered. By then we had already began having sex. I continued to cry in silence. A tear must have grazed his hand, because it was pitch dark. He would have not been able to see my face. "Are you crying?" Yes, I muffled. "You don't want to do this do you?" "NO," I whimpered." He stopped immediately, left the room and I never saw him again.

Yes, I have gone to hotels to meet people, driven hundreds of miles, and used up way too many minutes talking on my cell phone. Is it wrong to meet people online? Absolutely not! There are tons of people that do it every day and have wonderful friendships and relationships to show for it. It was not a good way for me to meet "Mr. Right" because my motive was so wrong. I finally became discouraged that I could not find my perfect match and I quit. I figured, if I am skipped over being chosen online by thousands of men, I guess nobody wants me. From this point on I considered myself "unlovable".

Dear Daughter,

You are free to be you. You are accepted. You are loved. Many people will not understand the calling on your life or the anointing that I have placed inside of you. I know it is very frustrating at times to be misunderstood. The enemy attempted to steal your gift early so you would not develop it. He knows the impact that you will have on the world when is finally revealed who you really are. Your year of being hidden is coming come to an end. It is time for the unveiling of your true identity. There will be one more major cut before the harvest. Listen closely. The enemy is trying to shout over me. Listen carefully through the shout of the enemy you will hear what I have to say clearly. There is an end to this chapter. Every end has a beginning. Your new assignment is on the way. I will begin to speak to you more and more. I LOVE YOU! I am with you today. I hold your heart right next to mine. Love is an action word, not a holiday. You can experience love on so many other levels than male/female. I AM love! Find ways to experience love with me on a daily basis. Stay on the potter's wheel. I am forming you. When I am finished you will finally see what I see. Gods Masterpiece!

One Love,

Your Father

Card #2

Dealing with Rejection

Daddy's Baby Mama's Maybe?

Drawing Dead

With This Ring

Happily Never After

Daddy's Baby, Mama's Maybe?

The year was 1999. Out of all the plans I had set out for my life having a baby was not one of them. I never wanted to have children because it would further deter me from living my life. I was already struggling to figure out who I was and what I wanted to do with my life! I had many aspirations at this point. I was still hoping to fly out to Dallas, TX and become a Dallas Cowgirl. The oldest qualifying age was 30 and I was only 19! So there was still time left. I was attending a local technical college now, but planned to transfer to an out of state college after my first year. I had also taken the big girl step of moving out living on my own. I was living "the good life". I was away from my aggravating mother! She was always hollering "if you don't like it then you can get out and get your own place", so I did. I made it to her goal of graduating high school without getting pregnant. I wanted to be independent, but I wanted more to be away from her and her husband. I admit I did not know much of anything, but I did know God would take care of me. I moved out with nothing but my clothing, and I was going to rebuild from there.

Finally! I was out on my own, working, going to college and of course, I had a boyfriend. A few years back I had finally conquered my search and met a guy. Nah, not online, but that was okay too. He was a nice guy, but most importantly he promised to protect me. He was somewhat rough around the edges, but he promised to always be there for me, he bought me anything I asked for, his only issue was religion, but I didn't care about that. I was tired of interviewing men. We met; I liked him, sort of. I grew to love him. Well, what I knew to be love. He had already told me he would never marry me, but I thought that would change when we got older. I understood people change their minds as they mature.

Congratulations Ms. Hunt! The test is positive. You are going to be a mother. Sitting in the doctors' office with a man who already made it clear he will never marry you, and the doctor congratulating you on a baby you really do not want, isn't the most exciting place to be. I cannot understand what happened because I

50

took every precautionary measure I could to not allow this to happen! Well, except the one that really works, which is not having sex at all! "Ms. Hunt, do you know what you want to do about the pregnancy?" The doctor asked. "What are my options?" I responded. "Well, if you choose not to keep the baby, you can give the baby up for adoption or terminate the pregnancy. However, in order to do so you only have about four more weeks to decide as you are already sixteen weeks along." "I knew it!" I chimed in. "I tried to tell everybody I was pregnant weeks ago, and nobody believed me. Urine test, after urine test showed negative. The only test that showed positive was a blood test, and now I only have 4 weeks to decide what to do?" "Yes Ms. Hunt. I'm sorry."

"She's going to keep it," he rumbled from across the other side of the room. The room shook from the low rumble that rushed from across the room, and I felt frozen in time. "Are you the child's father?" the doctor asked? "Yes, I am", he replied with an angry disposition. "With all due respect sir this decision is solely upon what is in the mother's best interest. She will ultimately make the decision." I thanked the doctor and bid him a good day. "You as well Ms. Hunt", he said as he exited the room. "If you kill this baby I will kill you", the father grimly stated. I had never felt fear like this before. Not from him. He had always protected me during our entire relationship. I never had reason to believe he would turn on me. He had never threatened me and always promised to protect me. I didn't even know what to say. Maybe he even knew that I was just being emotional. I didn't know much at that moment. I just knew I didn't want to die. So I guess my decision is made. I put my head down. I knew then, this was going to be a long road.

Why would God give me something I didn't ask for? The things I want the most are never in reach. I don't get it. I screamed, hollered, and cried, until I fell asleep. There are plenty of women in the world who would love to have children! I am not one of them. Negative thoughts began to permeate my mind. My sister was already 3 months pregnant and now I would have to tell my mother that she will have 2 grandchildren 3 months apart. Did I mention neither of us was married? Way to go Brandy! I said to myself. More shame that I would have to endure. That meant more judgment and persecution.

I waited for days to tell my mother. I agonized over the ridicule and embarrassment of being an unwed mother. I was rejecting the experience and my child before she was even born. I did not see one positive thing coming from this, and neither did anybody else apparently. My mother made it somewhat worse. By the time I conjured up enough nerve to tell her, she already knew. I guess that's a mom for you. The doctor sent a congratulatory letter home announcing the birth and what steps to take next. Being that I was on my mother's insurance it was addressed to her, not me so of course she opened it. My mom was very angry. I knew she would be as I came from a very judgmental family. It's not their fault though. I blame it on the modern day church. There is so much emphasis on what not to do when you get saved that they forget to teach that people will make mistakes. There should be more teaching on unconditional love, in my opinion.

My mother had very high expectations for me, and I was failing her by leaps and bounds. "Mom", I said, "I'm going to be fine. I have my own apartment; I have a job and a car. I think I am off to a pretty good start for a 19 year old." I was trying to be optimistic. "Brandy Michelle Hunt, you know better." Growing up, if mom said our middle name, we knew we were in big trouble! "Mom, God doesn't make mistakes right?" I was only trying to throw some church back at her. "That's what you taught me in church all my life," I said with authority and a slight attitude. "God didn't make the mistake, you did." Silence took over as tears streamed down my face. I didn't know what to do next, and I obviously didn't have my mother's support.

So, how do you expect me to love a child and I barely love myself? Not to mention I'm being forced to have it or it will mean my death? How are you so sure God didn't do this? I questioned God, a lot. There are plenty of women who would love to have a baby, why did you choose me? Why God? If my own mother doesn't support me, then why would I think anybody else would? I quickly became ashamed of the child I was carrying because I felt as if I would be frowned upon for having a child outside of marriage. The shame, guilt, embarrassment, judgment and ridicule that I faced inside my own head was almost unbearable.

As the months passed by the reality set in. I was really going to be a mother to somebody really soon. I prepared myself the best way I could for I knew the road was going to be long. I felt inadequate, incompetent, unprepared and alone. Not to mention, pregnancy life was horrible! I cannot remember a day that I was actually happy or content with who I was and what was taking place. I used to hear of women speaking about the "wonderful" pregnancy experience. I waited for it, it never came. I was overweight, miserable and uncomfortable! There was nothing pleasant about this experience!

Finally, the day arrived that she would enter the world and even that was tragic. My water had already broken. My epidural had been administered, but as my luck would have it, it didn't work. So I laid there in pain and agony from evening until the next morning. After much turmoil, pain and 15 hours of labor, she was absolutely refusing to make her entrance into the world. "Ms. Hunt, we will have to do a C-section", the doctor announced. Tears streamed down my face. Was I afraid of the surgery? No, I was upset that my dream of being a Dallas cowgirl would never come true, I would never get to wear a half shirt again, and I would have the ugly scar of this horrible experience to remind me of my mistake, as my mother called it. Thanks God.

We welcomed a bouncing 8 lbs 16 oz. baby girl. As I awoke from my gruesome surgery, with her father by my side, I would like to say I felt butterflies or some overwhelming sense of peace as some describe childbirth. But I didn't. I was in a lot of pain emotionally and physically. "Can I see my baby?" I asked. I looked down at what had to be the most precious and beautiful baby I had ever seen. Squinting at me with one eye open she looked at me, and I at her and I finally felt it. I felt a feeling I had never felt before. My anger went away. The animosity I was feeling about losing my "cheerleader dreams" vanished. I held a new dream in front of me. I was going to make sure this little girl knew that she had a mommy who loved her and would always be there for her. I looked down at her and said to her "Welcome to the World, Aniya Imani".

53

While we may not have known much about raising a baby, we knew we didn't want her to have some meaningless existence with a name that didn't mean anything; thus, Aniya means "a gift from God" and Imani means "faith". We chose for her a name that would at least be meaningful. If she ever lost me or forgot who she was she could revert back to her name. Even in the midst of how I felt about the situation and how other people made me feel, God chose to tell me in advance that she was indeed a gift sent from Him. Little did I know that I would constantly need this small reminder; she was his gift to me. She was not a curse or a mistake, but a gift. Imani would remind me that my faith would be the light to guide us throughout life's journey.

Drawing Dead

Drawing dead is a poker term used to describe a players'
current hand (situation). To be in a position that no card that
falls on any street could give a player a winning hand.
(pokerterms.com)

At this point in my life this is how I felt. No matter which
way I turned it was a dead end. A dead situation. My plan A, B,
and C had all been thrown out the window. Plan C had been to go
to the local technical college and work until I could transfer out to
a bigger college. This had all been halted by having a baby. This
little girl was now my responsibility. I began to blame my sorry
life and lack of success all on giving up my dreams. I was stopping
my life so she could live hers; not to mention her abusive father. I
would have to stop running the streets all the time. No more
clubbing, at least not all 3 days of the weekend, and my life was
over. I was tired of fighting with her daddy over my parenting
skills, or lack in his opinion, our relationship, and whatever else he
was angry about that day. I was tired of being fat and I was tired
of struggling to make ends meet. I had a very good job, but I was
very unfulfilled and unhappy. I never wanted to commit suicide
but I did contemplate running into a tree a time or two to get rid of
this horrible feeling of guilt.

A few years had gone by and I was settling into my new
role as "mother". Her father and I had decided by process of
elimination that he may not be a good fit for my life.

Well, let me tell the truth. He put his hands on me for the last and final time. So in essence, he decided.

One Christmas Eve, I left and stayed gone all day finishing up my last minute shopping. Upon my return home, he felt the need to express how angry he was because I had been gone all day, and he had stuff do and blah blah blah. I just let him talk though, but he had the nerve to be angry because I ignored him! I didn't care what he had to say. One swift blow and I was tumbling to the ground. He kicked me in my shoulder with his timberland boots on, in front of my two year old! It wasn't the first time he had roughed me up. But it was sure going to be the last. I got my baby and I left. This was one of those "aha" moments. I had already been praying to God to help me get out, so I wasn't even mad. I was relieved.

My friends wanted me to take a break from all the craziness. Our normal getaway location was Myrtle Beach, but this year we were going to Daytona Beach, FL! As I had recently gone back to the altar for the 10th time to rededicate my life to Christ, I felt as if I should not go. Not because I couldn't sin. That was never the case as I was never the "wild" beach goer. I was not going to be having sex with strangers or flashing my body parts to oncoming traffic. I just liked to go to have fun and enjoy the parties. At worst, I might flirt with somebody and maybe drink some alcohol, but never anything worse. I didn't listen to my gut, but I listened to my friends tell me how much fun it was going to be and that I would still be "saved". They kept reminding me of all the famous celebrities we would be seeing. Celebrities such as 50 Cent and Mario would be there as BET was filming "Rip the Runway" that year in Daytona Beach.

They convinced me that I was safe being with them. Well what do I have to lose I thought? It's just a beach. I knew I wasn't like those other girls. I was never one to show my goodies to the world outside of wearing some shorts or a skirt. I even packed "safe" clothing so that I appeared to be different. So after heavy anticipation, I ventured on to see if I could once again retrieve my "happy place".

Summer, summer, summer time! In the choral verse of the great Will Smith. I loved summer. I was super excited about our road trip and definitely ready to meet some new friends. We left South Carolina around midnight and arrived in Daytona Beach around 8:00a.m.

Now, let me add that I had been to Myrtle Beach Black Bike Week for about 3 years so I was accustomed to the heavy traffic, scantily clad women (I was not one of them), and lots of good looking men riding on motorcycles! It was a wonderful experience. It was like chocolate man heaven. But to my surprise it was NOTHING like Myrtle Beach. The traffic was 3 times as bad and the women were not just scantily clad, they were NAKED! I mean wearing nothing but pieces of dental floss they might refer to as a bathing suit. Oh well, we are here now, so we have to make the best of it. Almost immediately after checking into the hotel I felt a bit out of place. But as the old saying goes, just grin and bear it. So I did. My accompanying friends thought it best that our first stop be the "strip". For you non-beach goers, that is basically a 5 mile stretch of beach that houses thousands of pedestrians, their motorcycles, tents, and cars. At any given moment, regardless of time, there is a party going on outside. It's like a bar or better yet a night club without walls or time restrictions. Seems weird, but it doesn't take long to get accustomed to the environment.

After a few hours of prepping and primping as I like to call it we headed out the door to the land of good and plenty! We heard that 50 Cent was performing at the amphitheater a few miles away, so we headed in that direction. I was wearing a blue jean miniskirt with a thin tank top. It was a little revealing, but still "leaving something to the imagination" as my grandma used to say. In my opinion, I was still more covered than most of the women out there.

At the end of our 2 mile hike we finally made it to the main event and the concert was awesome! We even had front row access! I have always been a music lover regardless if it was R&B, gospel, rap, etc. There were so many people performing that I loved! So far we knew Ashanti, 50 Cent, and Mario would be on stage, just to name a few. "Ok, this might not be so bad after all. Let's run back to the room really quick and then go get something to eat so we can make it back for the next performance," one of my friends suggested. Ok, sounds good to me. So we ventured back down the 2 mile strip once more to get to our room.

"Well gang, it's about that time. We are going to miss the show if we are not leaving in the next few minutes." "This strip is surely getting longer every time we walk on it", I jokingly said as we briskly walked back to the amphitheatre. "Well baby let me carry you then", I heard just a few feet away. I looked up and in front of us stood a group of guys maybe 10 to 12 in a circle. They looked like they may have been talking amongst themselves and I failed to really identify where the voice came from either so I continued to walk. However, this group of men was standing right in our walking path on the sidewalk in our way! So my friends and I upon walking up on them said "excuse me". They decided not to move out the way, and before I could walk around them I was

58

snatched! I lost sight of my friends. It got dark. All of a sudden I was suspended in the air, but all I could see was men and hands. My legs were being pulled in different directions. Help! Somebody please help me! They began to rip my clothes off. I expected a large crowd of people to come to my rescue. Surely the police will come! They are on every corner. The police never came. I just kept praying "God please don't let them rape me out here". "Please don't let me die."

I heard some commotion and some random guys came to my rescue. They pulled the attackers off of me and hurried me back to their R.V. to shield me and get me to safety. Reluctant, I stood there at the door in shock. A young man gently put his arm around me and said "baby, it's going to be ok." He assured me that he was not there to hurt me, but to help me. "All men are not bad men", he said. I stood there mute, shaking. My friends resurfaced just in time, a bit shaken, but unharmed and we all went in together. I stood there in nothing but a bra, and a skirt. My shirt had been ripped to shreds, my flip flops where gone, and so was my dignity. "Why does this always happen to me?" I wailed. I wanted to go home! I knew I shouldn't have come! My friends were speechless. They didn't know what to say, or how to console me. They wanted to fight, but who were they going to fight? I could not have picked out those men in a line up. Where was law enforcement? Where was God? The walk back down the infamous "strip" was long, embarrassing, and shameful. It might as well have been the walk of death.

Every time I passed a police car I wanted to scream, cry, and report the incident. Every man I looked at was a rapist, molester, or gang member. I did manage to find a jacket to put over my bare chest. I didn't want any more visitors of the male persuasion groping on me and assuming that my nakedness was my permission to feel me up.

With tears in my eyes I swore to myself this was the last time I would be caught in a situation like this. This has happened way to many times. What am I doing wrong? Am I not "saved" enough? Does God not love me too? I had all these questions, and nobody had answers. I didn't want to ruin the rest of my friend's trip as we only had a day left so I spent the rest of the weekend slumbered away in the hotel room as they enjoyed beach life and I resorted back to the shame I had always known as "my life".

Drawing dead would have been the best term to describe how I was feeling at this point. There was not a good outcome I could come up with to the situations I have found myself in. What was the point of all these trials? Over the past 5 years I could not point out one good thing that happened to me. Not even the birth of my child could bring me joy because I was in so much pain. Every single time I try to do something, or have a goal to accomplish, something comes by and literally snatches it away from me! I quit! I absolutely refuse to do this anymore. God doesn't love me, because if he did he would have warned me or better yet, not let it happen.

With This Ring

As I studied the Bible more, and got to know God, not just religion and church, I began to feel like the street life was just not for me. Not because I didn't like it, because I did like it. I used to visit my aunt before I went out so she could pray for me. Weird huh? She would tell me God had a call on my life and one day he was going to use me, but I didn't see it, or understood what she meant. The more she said it, the more I began to feel something change inside me. I started to feel like there was more to life than what I had been living.

Often, I thought to myself that my quest for "Mr. Right Now" was leaving me with too many bad experiences. With all that I had to gone through, I was still trying to run with the world but stay in line with the church and it had been too much for me to handle. I was tired emotionally, physically, and spiritually. I guess the Bible was right when it talked about not being conformed to this world but being transformed by the renewing of your mind! This world will turn you out and quickly. It is always leaving you to pick up the pieces by yourself. Everybody is with you when you are living wrong; try to start living right and see how many friends you lose.

The church folks always talk about how much "marriage works" and how that's the ultimate goal. I thought maybe God is trying to send me a husband and I'm missing the big picture. So maybe I should just stop dating and start waiting for my husband. Sounds good right? Fabulous, in fact!

In a perfect world or at singles ministry conference, yeah! Though "being single and ready to mingle" sounds much better than "being still and waiting". At least to me it did; but since I had turned over a new leaf in my life, and was now serving God for real this time, I decided to do things His way. My way definitely did not profit me; unless you count heartache, pain, and bitterness as profit. Well, in that case I was rich.

Now, I do not know about you, but when you go from dating whoever asks first to waiting and letting "God bring you the man" the first thing that comes your way is a breath of fresh air. Waiting is going to give you a lot of time between men, unlike when you are saying yes to everything that breathes you are on a constant revolving door of dating heaven. It's like being stuffed in a closet and then someone suddenly opens the door. Though I know every day has 24 hours, some of the waiting days and nights felt sooo long! I have never known what chemistry creates the desire and attraction between men and women, but it's something fierce!

Anyway, about a year into my "waiting game" a church friend of mine said he had a friend that was single and looking to wife somebody up and wanted to know if I would be interested in meeting him. "Well, let me check this long line of men I have knocking my door down and let me get back to you", I said sarcastically. "Of course, I will meet him!" Shoot, I been locked up for over a year "waiting", I thought to myself. Remember, I was the blind date queen, so this was at least a step up! It was safer. At least his friend knew who he was and I trusted his judgment as he was a minister at the church. I happily obliged and agreed it was ok to give him my number.

He called me later that evening. It was wonderful! He didn't bombard me with sex talk, he talked about more than himself, and he actually held my attention, which is very hard for some guys to do. So far so good! We decided to meet in person a few days later. We went on a group date with some other singles, so that was even better! Thus if I didn't like him, or vice versa, there were other people we could talk to and it would not be so awkward. Thankfully we didn't need the others. Did we hit it off? Of course! He was a godly man, saved, sanctified, holy ghost filled, fire baptized and on his way to heaven, JUST LIKE ME! He didn't want to have sex until marriage, JUST LIKE ME! Glory to God! I have found the one. This must be God! All that praying, fasting and waiting has surely paid off!

A few months later we were having the "marriage" talk. He said "I'm going to make you my wife one day." My heart did a flip. This must be God! I prayed and he has answered. Now I know it has only been 3 months, but it's been a good 3 months. We have been as saved as humanly possible. We did not have sex, even though I tried to tempt him many times. Try not to judge me; let me explain. The lifestyle and experiences that I had gone through led me to believe the only way to know if a man really wants you is if he wants to have sex with you. I was often skeptical if he really loved me because he said he wanted to do it the "right way."

I quickly responded to the "I'm going to marry you" statement. "Well what are you waiting for? We aren't getting any younger." We were only about 24 years old at the time. "Do you want to marry me or not?" I asked. I have a very strong personality and at times I might have even been rather intimidating . "Yes of course", he responded. "Then it's a go right? I could care less if you have a ring right now. That doesn't matter to me", I quickly persuaded him. He agreed and that was how our engagement began.

I know what you are thinking. Brandy, you should have not been so aggressive. Never marry a man that doesn't have a ring. Yeah, yeah, you may be right, but my mind was telling me to do it, FAST and NOW!

Where did this attitude of persuasion come from? What was I dealing with at the time? I honestly believe I was trying to redeem the bad marks that had been placed on my life, by other people. I needed something good to happen to me to erase all the negatives that I had been dealing with for so long. What's better than a wedding? Everybody loves weddings! Finally I would be praised and celebrated instead of being rejected and talked about. My mother would be so proud of me for picking a good guy and I would have gotten my "picture perfect" card back.

It was December and we were planning for a May wedding. Still with no engagement ring in sight, I was diligent in planning. We went to visit his parents for the holidays and tell our "big news" in person. But he never said anything, to anybody. I pulled him to the side once we were alone. "Why are you not saying anything about the wedding to your family? Are you ashamed of me?" He was a very quiet person, not argumentative so his answer was very simple. "I just wasn't ready to tell them". I actually shrugged it off as pre-wedding jitters and continued planning.

Did you know your bad motives tend to only take you to one place? Nowhere. I will admit I loved him but we had only been together about 5 months at this point. I know now, that I was only doing it to get brownie points with my family and I would have failed at being a wife. Even if I didn't want to admit it, I wasn't ready. I was still broken inside from some of the things I had gone through, but I figured I will fake it till I make it!

Up to this point I had not ever heard God's voice. I was sitting in church one Sunday morning and I heard these words ever so clearly "I'm not trying to take something from you; I'm trying to get something to you". What? God? Was that you? I was confused. The voices in my head were always negative statements about how horrible I was and how much my life was a mess. I wrote it down anyway as it was the first thing I had ever heard God speak to me. I went on with my Sunday.

Later that evening I received a call from my beloved fiancé'. He said "Brandy, we need to talk". Ok, let's talk. Men do not normally say that, so when you hear a man say that, you should be listening intently. He said these words "I'm not ready to get married". As soon as he said it, God's voice spoke again in a whisper, Brandy, "I'm not trying to take something from you, and I'm trying to get something to you". Well God, what is it this time? You are going to take him from me aren't you? Before I even get to experience this bliss of our relationship? I was speechless. However, since I had heard God's voice, I had peace and an overwhelming sense that everything would be alright. He went on to say he would fast and pray about it for a week. During this time we would not speak to each other as that would cloud his judgment and we will see if his decision changes.

The end of the week came, and so did the end of our relationship. I prayed hard. Nothing changed. He called back and said not only did he not want to get married but he didn't even want to be boyfriend and girlfriend anymore. "Why? What did I do?" I cried. "Nothing", he replied sweetly. "It's nothing you did. I should have stopped you from wedding planning a long time ago. You just looked so happy." "Do you realize that I have bought a wedding dress that is NON-refundable? My bridesmaids have paid for their dresses! I let go of my apartment and moved in with my aunt and her family to save money just to pay for this wedding! Does my sacrifice not mean anything?" "I understand Brandy, but this is the way I feel, and nobody can change that", he said in a low whisper. "I love you, I just do not want to hurt you by marrying you and I'm not ready."

I hung up the phone in utter disbelief. Reality struck me instantly. I would have to face my family to tell them about yet another failure in my life. I am never planning anything again! I am not setting anymore goals. For what? I'm surely at Plan D by now and yet again another failure. Again I took my fathers' advice and chose not to let the situation make me bitter, but to learn from it. At this point I'm not sure what the lesson was, but I sure wasn't going to let one monkey stop this show. I chose to begin to focus on more prevalent things like my career, and I moved on with my life.

Has there ever been a time in your life when you wanted to just throw everything down and start fresh? Well that's exactly what I wanted. Where else can you go but up once you have reached your dead end? Even though I didn't feel God I still prayed and ask God to guide my footsteps. I knew deep inside he still had a plan. As the old saying goes "sometimes you have to lose to win".

Due to circumstances beyond my control I found myself without a job. I had been at this company for about 5 years, and due to an illness I had been battling that resulted in multiple absences, they let me go. Another major upset. But still I pressed on.

I quickly found employment within another company, even though it wasn't my first pick; I did it with a smile on my face. I knew God had an amazing plan for my life. He had to, because at this point I was all out of options and plans. So let's recap the hand I was dealing with so far; in the past 11 years my father died, I was molested, raped, busted my knee, had to have major surgery, missed college, had a baby out of wedlock, been ganged by 10 men, left at the altar and fired from my job. These may not be major let downs to you, but they were to me. I felt crushed. No, I do not have another plan. And at this point I wasn't really sure if God even cared.

Happily Never After

I have often heard stories of how God had to get people alone so that he could deal with them, or maybe teach them something, change their character. There are times He needs to get you away from the noise and the voices so you can hear from Him clearly what His will is for your life. So on that note: Brandy Hunt, get ready to move to Atlanta, GA.

Atlanta, home of the Braves. Atlanta may have the Braves, but Brandy was afraid. When I heard the voice of God speak to me to tell me to move to Atlanta I was terrified! For the past 10 years, I had only lived in Greenville, SC; this would definitely be a season of faith not fear.

When God gives you a vision, He will make the provision. God gave me a specific move date and confirmed Himself every step of the way! Even down to causing other people to bless me. My aunt believed in me so much that she obeyed God and gave me a car that she had just purchased cash! It was already paid for and was only about 5 years old! I got a job and found housing all by the move date that God had shown me from the beginning. While I was in Atlanta I was in Gods favorite class, Faith Building 101. It definitely taught me how to rely on God. Satan does not care about your geographical location. He is going to continue to try you until your break. Again, I was there by myself. My daughter stayed in Greenville while I got things together in Atlanta. Talk about faith! I even had to leave my child behind in order to trust God, but He saw me the entire way through. After of few months of residing in Atlanta, my biggest test of faith had to be the day when I was driving from getting my brakes changed.

I was having trouble getting my tag transferred to Atlanta from Greenville, but I continued to drive without one. I didn't know it was illegal. Call me ignorant, but that's why women have men in their lives. I just drive cars. I never learned anything else about them. Anyway, as I was on my way to the bank to cash my paycheck and get my tag situation cleared up a police car pulled up behind me and blue lighted me. This was the second time I had been stopped so I figured I would just explain to the officer why my tag was missing, like I did with the first one. "License and registration please". "Here you go officer", handing him my information. "Do you know why I stopped you?" "Yes, my tag is missing. But I'm on my way to get it fixed now. I'm from out of town and I'm having trouble getting it transferred." "Very likely story Ms. Hunt, but okay". He went to his car. He returned a few minutes' later and said the worst words I could have ever heard. "Please step out the car Ms. Hunt; I am going to have to arrest you". What the???? "Why?" I responded quickly. "Yes your tag is missing, but also your license is suspended for failure to pay a ticket in South Carolina." "Whaaaat! I have never gone without paying my tickets." "I understand Ms. Hunt. But you will have to come with me and clear it up from the jail".

And well, you know the rest. I was experienced embarrassment, rejection, dishonor, disappointment, and just downright angry. God, please help me. I am here by myself. You gave me this stupid car, now you going to curse me with what you blessed me with! The devil is a liar! Who is going to come bail me out? Who is going to believe I am in jail first of all? I rode in the back of the police car in utter amazement. When people passed by they seemed to look at me with the most discontent. I'm thinking to myself, I am not a criminal. But it didn't matter. Being

69

in the back of that police car made me one. I arrived at the jail and was finger printed and patted down. Talk about humiliation! This had to be one of the worst experiences of my life. They left me in a square block with four walls, a wooden bench and a telephone. I didn't know what to do first. Crying felt like a good place to start. However, it was not going to get me out of that cinder block any faster. I began to call on the name of Jesus. That's all I knew. God showed me who to call and about 8 hours later, I was released.

I stayed about 6 more months and after that God released me to come back to Greenville, SC. During my 1 year there it was difficult being alone, but the greatest lesson I learned was how to trust in God, not people. People tend to fail you at times. But God will never fail you. When nobody else could be there, God was there.

Atlanta, we had a great run, but thank God I was moving back to the Carolinas where I had friends, family and a good support system.

Now, here is another twist to this already bizarre story. I was given a prophetic word that my husband was soon to come; they even gave me his name. At this point I was in shock because the name they gave was of the man that I had been engaged to and still had deep feelings for. I will add that this prophecy came from a 5 year old. Try not to judge me. (LOL) I was excited, but still trying to use wisdom; I put it on the shelf in my mind. I still didn't have that husband I was looking for, but it was alright. I was a bit more settled in my life as I was about 28 years old. I discovered some new aspects of me and I was genuinely happy with who I was becoming. I had more faith than fear thanks to my trip to Atlanta. However, I'm sure you can relate that lonely feeling creeps up on you rather quickly.

After the "prophecy" I thought I should reach out to my ex and see if there was anything that was still able to be rekindled. I figured I would just give God a little help. I had been gone out of the state for over a year, but before I left we had spent the day together, so maybe, just maybe? We were older now, and surely it wouldn't hurt to just say hello to an old friend, right? I spoke with him over the phone and he happily obliged. Sure! Come on over, it will be great to catch up with you. Total disaster! The feelings I expected to be there were not there, on either side. As a matter of fact there was more hostility in the air than an Iraqi hostage situation. I left in tears. The man I knew and loved was no longer standing in front of me. I knew how I wanted to be loved and he was failing me by leaps and bounds. I was definitely not marrying him; I do not care what the prophecy said. I refused to allow my past to still bring me pain and I refused to settle for less! I walked out the door knowing this time, it was for good.

I called my friend in tears. "It's ok Bran", as my friend affectionately calls me, "you should call the chat line." That will cheer you up. You just want somebody to talk to right? I just met this guy and he seems to be pretty cool. Pause for a moment. Let's take a visit back to card # 1-www.foolishness.com. You do know I was a pro at blind dates, right! But up to this point they lead to nothing good. Technically, the man I loved started as a blind date! I even tried it when I was in Atlanta - pure, unadulterated, foolishness. I met a few guys but nothing that led anywhere. I have gone through more blind date experiences gone wrong than I have time to write about in this book.

"No friend", I replied. "I will not do it. Those guys only want one thing. SEX! Absolutely not, I repeated". "Well here is the number, just in case you change your mind", she said with a grin and giggle. "Whatever, I'm too focused right now to be fooling with somebody who doesn't want a future. I want a husband. I want what God promised me. That's my final answer".

Well, temptation got the best of me and two days later I was on the chat line. Call me what you want. I had a weak moment! Do not be fooled, it was just as I had suspected. After a few failed attempts, to my surprise, I did come across an individual who could have a conversation without talking about sex every other sentence. The scariest part was this individual I had the "connection" with had the same name as my ex! I remembered the prophecy at first, but put it to the back of my mind. This was just too easy. But one and one started to equal 2. He attended the same church I went to, had been to the same School of Arts, and lived in some of the same cities. Even though we had much in common, I thought, I probably shouldn't even be talking to you, but we will give it a try. I forgot the "system" is designed to "match" you with people who fit your profile description. They got me! The next day we decided to meet up.

The initial meeting went from bad to worse instantly. He called and said I do not want to cancel, but my car broke down. Do you think you could pick me up? Well, with me being the kind hearted, compassionate human being that I am replied, "Sure"! "Oh and can you pick up my kids too". Really dude? Fine, no problem. Yes, the first date was me, him, his two children and my one. But it was the sweetest feeling! It was just like a family. The exact picture of what I had always wanted. Aside from the car breakdown, the day was perfect. We all meshed, it felt like a real family. By the end of the day he had met my mother, I met his and even his kid's mother. This was moving at the speed of light! But hey God, if you are cool with it, then so am I.

We ended the evening by dropping off the kids and heading downtown Greenville to the waterfall. This is where all the couples go who are in love. On any given day you may see couples holding hands, kissing, and my favorite, taking wedding photos. We found an intimate spot on one of the big rocks. As I lay in his arms the wind blew through my hair and I exhaled; finally, someone who understands me. As we continued to talk we became engulfed in each other and it was if we were the only ones there. It was almost surreal.

I usually hate first dates. They are so fake and uncomfortable. People can act so uptight sometimes. The constantly try to be fake instead of just showing who they genuinely are. The night dew was beginning to fall and the sun was setting in the east. It was getting a little chilly and he wrapped his arms around me to show me how masculine he was. It worked. I felt comfortable. We felt like "we fit". We talked for what seemed like hours about where we had been in life and where we wanted to go. He even put the icing on the cake. Let's go to church together tomorrow! Hold up, wait a minute. Growing up, that's when you really knew somebody was for real, when they brought their man to church. Deal! Yeah, I know I need to pick you up right? But it's cool. Everybody falls on hard times. You said your car is in the shop, so no big deal. The evening faded and we went our separate ways.

I woke up excited about my new found love and off to church we went, and now the fairytale begins:

The bright sun was peeking through the trees that swayed above us on this beautiful breezy August afternoon. As the sunrays kissed our chocolate brown skin we gazed into each

other's eyes. Strolling through the front yard of my mother's
house 2 days after we met, standing toe to toe and gazing past
my eyes he speaks to my soul. In his freshly creased church
pants he kneels down on the gravel driveway and nervously
utters these words: I know we just met, but I believe we were
meant to be together. Will you marry me? Whaaaaaaaaat!!!!
Only in the fairy tales right? Boy meets girl, they fall in love,
and they get married! I rationalized it in my mind. Wow, a
man that will get dirty for me. That's awesome. First I said no,
then my other brain kicked in and said, well God said he was
sending me a husband named (insert name here). The man I
thought it would be doesn't want me. Here is a man on his
knee proclaiming his undying love for me. Yeah I know it has
only been two days, but he deserves a chance! I mean he's
cute. He had a few obstacles working against him, but nothing
I had not successfully handled previously.
 Besides, with all I have been through, his problems were
miniscule. I just refuse to let this one get away! THIS MUST
BE GOD! So I said YES! I'm finally going to get my
husband!

I know what you're thinking. How could you say yes to
marrying a man you have only known for 2 ½ days! But I'm
an optimist. Sometimes rejection makes you do things that you
would not normally do. I know how it feels to be rejected. I
could not stomach telling that man no at that moment. Maybe
later, but I could not crush him like that. When you walk
around with the spirit of rejection any type of acceptance
makes you jump at the first thought of someone wanting you.
Rejection is the root of all issues. Abandonment, anger,
emptiness, forgiveness and the list goes on. When you feel

unwanted, unloved and unappreciated, you are in a dangerous place within yourself. Rejection is what causes people to commit suicide. Rejection is what causes women to stay in an abusive relationship when they know better.

We were so happy, we ran into the house to tell my mother what had just happened. From the look on her face, this was going to be another "Mom, I'm pregnant" moment. She did not look happy at all. She asked him why he wanted to marry me, and how he would take care of me and my child. I believe she was genuinely concerned. I believe she would have been happy for me eventually, but after 2 days she just couldn't see the cup half full with me. I just wanted her to be happy for me. After Atlanta's gut wrenching faith walk and my heart being broken by that other guy, I was just excited that something good was happening to me! But she is a mom and sometimes mom see what you refuse to admit already exists. "Well that's okay mom. You will see. We will be fine." We ventured on into the land of pre-wedding bliss in our newly discovered 2 ½ day love.

Dear Daughter,

Your greatest power is the power to choose. Choosing requires faith. I believe in you. I trust you to carry out the assignment I have placed on your life. I gave you your dreams and I intend to see them come to fruition. Trust in me. Not just for material things. I promise that you will have everything you need. Trust in my good plan for

Your life. Trust in my word. I have hidden you because you are a precious jewel to me. Just as I have in the past, I will turn this situation around to work out for your good. You are victorious over every circumstance you are faced with. I love you. You shall lack no good thing in your life. My promises are yes and amen. I will cover you with my feathers; under my wings you can take refuge. I am a safe place. I will guard you in all your ways. You are closer than you think you are. I love you more than you know. With great care I knit you together. When I thought of what a masterpiece would look like, I created you. Don't give up when it looks like all is lost. My promises are yes, and amen.

               With Everlasting Love,

               Your Father

Card # 3

Dealing with Fear

Poker Face

Can You See Me Now

The Little Engine that Shoulda

Poker Face

Poker face, as defined by dictionary.com, is a blank face or blank expression of one who is an **expert** *at concealing his/her true emotions.*

In the card game of poker, this term is used to describe a defensive strategy. This happens whenever a player wants to disguise the true identity of the hand they have been dealt. In doing this they display the opposite of the truth. His lack of smiling may indicate he has a bad hand, when indeed he has a good hand. And vice-versa, he may be smiling, but have a bad hand. It is the player's intent to deceive you into thinking his hand is one way, when in actuality it's another.

We as women are EXPERTS at this!! I have had to go through some of the toughest times with a smile on my face. I didn't want the world to know I had issues too, so I hid them behind a smile, achievements, and busyness. We are the great pretenders. I can imagine the confusion our hearts and minds go through on a daily basis. In this day and age, everybody doesn't need to know your business. People are nosey and sometimes just want to know your business so they can use you for "table talk" later. However, you also are not required to be "blessed and highly favored" when you are clearly "angry and highly annoyed".

During my worst trials there were moments I have just wanted to crawl under a pew, or sprout wings and fly to better days! I just wanted to pretend that I and my problems never existed! How about let me wear a "perfect" mask so I could pretend like I didn't have problems or failures in my life. I had tons of other masks too. The "everything is ok mask", "no, I do not need help" mask, and my favorite, "no, I'm not hurting" mask. Those were just a few of the top ones I hid my shame behind. If you are anything like me I bet you have perfected the "poker face" too.

Several moments in my life have had shameful parts, but nothing I couldn't bounce back from; until now. Like any human being, I have been ashamed of something I had done, but I swept up the mess and kept going. That was not going to happen this time. This one wouldn't shake quite like the others. It was big and messy, and spilling over into every area of my life. It was inevitable that someone would see the mess that I had created with my life and start asking questions.

It all started after my Cinderella moment. I should have known it was too good to be true! I wanted to recreate the feeling of having a family. I just wanted to be "normal." Family means everything to me. I grew up with a large family. But circumstances and life events began to draw us apart. I carried a void that I didn't notice was there. One of my favorite memories growing up as a child was eating at the dinner table with my entire family. I loved Sundays the most because it meant that we would be going to church as a family. After church my mom would be in the kitchen cooking and we would be playing around the house waiting for dinner to finish or at least trying to help her. I really wanted that moment back more than anything. That was my "happy place". To feel like a family again, I wanted to allow my daughter to experience the love of a mother and father under the same roof.

I had perfected the poker face. I had to. There were so many people who were depending on me to make it, so failure was not an option. Even though my life was a mess, I couldn't emotionally deal with one more label or statistic. I was a broken individual trying to piece together what I could and call it whole. But two broken people will not create anything whole; but a whole lot of mess! I was most embarrassed to show my face to my family because they were the ones I was trying to please.

Growing up, there was always an unspoken rule. Get it right, or get laughed at, ridiculed, or picked on. God knows I didn't want any of those responses so I did what I could to keep it together.

I will admit they tried to show me "warning signs" before, during and after. However, I have always been strong willed so of course, I had to see for myself. And boy did I see. I believe at one point God himself even tried to stop me. How do I know you ask? Well, I had a dream before we got married that he had on a wedding dress and I had on the tuxedo. When I woke up I immediately panicked! I said, "oh God! He's gay!" God quickly responded, "No he is not gay; your relationship is out of order". I called one of my friends and she quickly confirmed the same thing God told me. Being the "fixer" that I am, I sought out marriage counseling. I wanted it to happen so badly! My motto is, if it's broke, fix it and keep on moving. "And if it does not fix now, bring it with you, maybe you can fix it along the way." This was "normal" to me. I was used to bringing home the bacon, frying it up in the pan and wearing 6" stilettos while I served it up.

As I look back I do not believe this was Gods intention for my life. I was overworked and receiving heart ache after heart break and I was married and still hurting. That was definitely not in the plan. I was worn down, but nobody knew. How could I let people see that my Cinderella story was over and my glass slipper had shattered into a billion tiny unrecognizable pieces? The grand finale wedding we had put on was beautiful, but 2 days after the wedding I was talking to his side chicks, not 1 but 2? How could I possibly tell anybody that I was fist fighting my husband 3 months into our marriage? Well I did try to tell somebody. Unfortunately, all I received was more hurt and rejection. It hurt more because it was church folk! I was told that I could not be a part of a ministry at church because of what I was going through at home. There was no counseling was offered, no prayer lines formed. "That's fine; I don't want to be a part of your ministry if that's how you treat hurting people."

I refused to allow anybody to see that I had messed up. My poker face was not just a mask. I got to a point where it was a permanent fixture to my face. It was who I had become. Who was I behind the mask? I was abandoned, rejected, angry, bitter, selfish, and cold. Outside the mask I was friendly, all smiles and full of happiness. The mask was attached to my face. I could not find enough strength to walk in the truth, so I lived a lie. I did not know who I was, so I continued to fabricate who I was not to get people to like me. I used my pretty smile and acting skills to help create an image good enough to hide behind. I preferred to be a "fake" and accepted by man than to be rejected by man and healed by God.

Fortunately, there are some real men and women of God in this world who can see past the fakeness, into my pain. You may hide from people for a while, but you won't get by with hiding from God for very long. Especially when you know he has told you specifically not to do something, and you go against his will. I was hurting so bad. I just wanted out and I didn't know how to get out. God is faithful, and even though I didn't know who I was or where I was going, He did.

My husband was not what one thinks of as a typical physical abuser but more like public embarrassment, yelling, and some cowardly pushing. I would like to interject here that there is not ever a time where abuse is allowable. If you are in a relationship that is not healthy, loving and Godly, get out in a hurry. Abuse is never right. It can be emotional, physical, or financial. My point is that it would have been easier for me to have an excuse to run away from a relationship where he was slapping me around or punching me in my face. That's not what was happening, so I figured "dealing with it" meant staying and tolerating it.

I was constantly disrespected on a regular basis and there were way too many women in my marriage! I recall the time where I went through the cell phone bill and called a few numbers. Something just wasn't adding up. Yes, I am Sherlock Holmes! I may have missed my calling as a private detective. I wanted to get to the truth.

After calling a few numbers I spoke with several women who confirmed what I already knew to be true. One woman admitted she had been conversing with my husband for about 3 months and he was making promises of being with her. When confronted about it you know what he said? Ironically, he admitted it, but blamed me! He thought I was going to leave him, so he was securing his back-up plan, I guess. I should have listened to my gut, stopped making threats and left like I should have. Women's intuition is something serious!

Ladies, there comes a time in life where you just have to "call a spade a spade". I was trying to convince myself it wasn't exactly what it was! Most women at this point are probably thinking "you should have packed up that day"! But, again I didn't want the label of divorce. I wanted so badly for God to fix it! Though, why would he fix something he told me not to touch in the first place? I had already been a statistic of being an unwed mother, I didn't want to be called a divorcee too, and on top of that a statistic of domestic violence? OOOOHHHH NOOOOO! I decided I would hang in there just a little while longer. That's what most of my Christian advisers told me to do anyway.

I prayed and fasted, fasted and prayed. I probably called down a thousand angels a million times! I had to keep convincing myself that this was going to get better. People would say things like: "He was just stressed out. Men get stressed out when they are not working and it was going to get better. Pray for him."

Check, check, and check. I had done all those things! I finally had to result to a place of reality, which was this; I do not care if a man doesn't have a job, it is never right for him to take his anger out on anyone. I finally began to love myself enough to stop tolerating mess! Secondly, when you are married, not coming home at night is not an option unless you are working 3rd shift, which he was not. He was not ready to be a provider and I was tired of doing everything! I might as well have been the man in the relationship. I was carrying things that I didn't have the strength for and I was worn out. I was a single mother of one child when I met him, and now I have 2, my daughter and my husband. Not to mention I had to share him with 3 other women (that I knew of). From what I recall, my marriage vows did not include sharing my husband with someone else.

Please understand that I believe in the power of prayer, but I also believe in the power of get somewhere and sit down, deal with your issues, and let God heal you. Sometimes you can heal the marriage in the same home, and sometimes you cannot. Let

God show you the best option for your marriage. For me, the situation was obviously getting worse by the day and there was nothing God was going to do until I chose to stop it. Why? Because God gives us free will. We have the greatest power on earth which is the power to choose. For a person dealing with abandonment making the decision to leave them is going to be awfully painful. It requires that you feel that feeling again of rejection and aloneness that we so often try to avoid. That's nothing but fear. It's not the abandonment that bothers you. It's the fear of being alone, again. But I would rather be happy and alone, than in a relationship that is falling apart daily.

I'm not saying that I was perfect and he was worthless. As a matter of fact, if he ever read this book I would hope he would value the things I said about him that were good. I sincerely believe he was in a place of pain, rejection, abandonment, and anger just as I was. When we married we were both scarred from our past. Early on, because of my mentors and influences I found ways to better myself so I did have much more to offer spiritually, emotionally, and financially. That didn't make me a better Christian or any closer to God, I just knew from where to get the help I needed to succeed.

I have always been one to learn from my issues and get past them than to dwell on them and let them keep me down. He on the other hand was quite the opposite. His mother told him constantly he was stupid and would never be anybody. She often pushed him around and abused him. He was abused, so he abused. He also believed what he heard spoken over his life about himself, and so he became every lie he believed. Now here we are, two people who are clueless about their individual identity and are now married and damaging one another's lives at a rapid pace. It's a very vicious cycle. It must be broken, before somebody gets seriously hurt. Will you break the cycle?

I knew from the beginning these relational issues existed and I ignored them believing that if "he put a ring on it", that would magically make a family. I knew in my heart he would eventually become the man I needed him to be. I had finally done it "right" according to the church. I waited on God, a man proposed to me. We did our best to not have sex before we got married and got married quickly so that we would not "live in sin" as the church folk called it. I had reached my goal of making my family proud of me. The wedding was beautiful and everything looked "perfect". On the outside anyway.

Somewhere in the good book, the BIBLE, it says all I had to do was get married and God would do the rest, at least that's what I was made to believe.

Comments like; he is a man he will grow out of it, and just pray, started to become mundane. I was out of prayers and I was losing myself and my mate to the lack of integrity, no holiness in my marriage, anger, bitterness, rage and the list goes on.

My "poker face" was slowly becoming tired face, angry face, despair face, fake it till you make it face, and I desperately desire to not take this anymore face! I was so beat down. My heart was so broken. Who can mend a broken heart? My husband couldn't. We even separated for a season and that seemed to make it worse. People would often look at me and ask what was wrong? I just would say "nothing" because it was easier. I didn't want to dump my life's issues into somebody else's lap only to end up with the same answers, but I had to tell somebody. I needed anybody that would listen and tell me something other than "God's going to fix it." "Is he going to fix it before we kill each other?" was always my response.

I know the bible says God hates divorce. Do you believe he hates two people destroying each other's character every chance they get and by any means necessary? "I want out right NOW!" I screamed and cried as I confided in my friend. I just had no idea where to go. I prayed and asked God to get me out. I promised God I would go the way He was leading and I would not deter from it if he showed me exactly what to do. Surprisingly, a few days later my response came. Leave your husband in Georgia. What?

I was used to people leaving me. So when the word of the Lord came to pack my things and journey back to South Carolina with only my child and my belongings my heart sank. Yes, I had to leave my husband. I was devastated. Of course my brain said, but God doesn't like divorce. I was quickly reminded by the still small voice that he didn't like chaos either. We were in a mess. My husband even admitted to me that if we didn't have a license keeping us together he would have walked away a long time ago.

That moment took me back to my childhood. I believed my father thought I was too much, so that's why he committed suicide. My step-father left one day and never came back. In my mind, that said you are too much to handle.

And now, here is my husband haunting me with the same words. You do too much, you know too much of the bible, you are too much to handle. When he found out about "the prophecy" he felt obligated to marry me, just as did I. I was the more spiritual of the two of us so he repeatedly admitted he depended on me to lead us. I was disobedient in marrying him. I could have said no, but the pain and anguish that came from the feelings of abandonment and rejection were unbearable. What will people think if I did not come down the aisle? I had one engagement cancelled, I'm not cancelling another. These and all sorts of negative thoughts flood my mind. I didn't want to have to feel that abandoned and lonely feeling again.

I'm no marriage expert but I do know marriage is a growing together process, and we were quickly tearing each other apart every chance we could.

The day I decided to leave. I crept away like a thief in the night. I was so ashamed. I was not one to leave people. I knew what abandonment felt like and I didn't want to do it, but I didn't have a choice. I had to get to safety.

God is always in our midst. Regardless of how bad we may have messed up in a situation He has not turned His back on us. I knew that in order to do this God would have to show me the way.

Even though I had begged for a way out, now that it was time, I was afraid. I didn't know how this was going to end. I really loved this man, but I finally loved myself more. I was finally coming into knowing who I was, and what I wanted, and I wasn't afraid to say it. I was tired of asking about other women. When I looked to my future I didn't see us together.

As our history included a knock down drag out fight with him once before, I was afraid of what his response would be if I told him I was leaving him. He depended on me for everything but air. I mean, I was his wife. This was supposed to be until death do us part right? He wasn't going to just let me leave because I wanted to even though he admitted to not wanting to be with me. So I didn't tell him. I let him believe I was going to a homeless shelter. At the time we were trying to transition and we were staying with some friends in Atlanta. I know you asking, how did

I manage to let him convince me to move back there? I was so nervous but I had to do it.

I let him help me pack as he thought that we were all going to the homeless shelter. As we loaded the final belongings in the car I prayed, God how am I going to leave him? He is not going to let me go. I got in the drivers' seat and sat there trying to devise a plan. At that moment, my friend's dog ran out the house and he ran after it and I left. Yes, my way of escape. I do not advise you do anything that would put your life in immediate danger. This is just how God directed me to leave. Desperate and afraid I followed the direction of the Lord. I had no money so I called some friends and also pawned my wedding ring too. What good would it be to me now?

I arrived back in South Carolina heartbroken and afraid, but safe. A good friend of mine allowed me to stay at her home until God showed me what to do next. We sat down and talked and she and her husband agreed to keep my child, but I could not stay. She wanted me to go get help at a domestic violence shelter. I could have felt rejected, but I knew God was turning things around. Funny thing about God, He will show you glimpses of your future. They may seem farfetched at the moment, but when it happens you won't be surprised. God had shown me that I was going to go into a shelter. I thought it would be a homeless shelter, but it ended up being a domestic violence shelter.

They drove me in the police car to the secluded shelter, I was terrified. This ride was quite different. I wasn't in handcuffs, but the questions that flooded my mind were the same and God's answer was the same. What have I done to deserve such drastic measures? God is there any other way we can do this I asked? A still small voice spoke to me, "this is my will for your life, and I am with you."

Can you imagine the devastation I was feeling? In a matter of 5 days I lost my husband, I planted my child somewhere safe while I rebuilt my life, not to mention my car was repossessed while I was pumping gas one day, I was unemployed and my new address had barbed wire fence around it. I didn't know how I was going to start over. I had nothing to start over with. I was ashamed to call on my family. It was going to be so embarrassing to look them in the face. I did not want to deal with the ridicule, finger pointing, and "I told you so". I decided I was going to do this on my own and when they hear about it, it will be a thing of the past. Just God and me; and based on past experiences, I knew that they would call me a failure.

I was already broken; I could not face the possibility of being kicked while I was already down. I could find no value in myself and I was using previous situations and circumstances to calculate my worth. My Ex used to say nobody would want me because I had a child and now I was going to be a used up thrown away divorcee. No one wants a woman that the first man didn't want.

On a scale of 1-10, I was worth about a -25 in my eyes. I had nothing to be proud of and nobody to tell me that everything was ok. I had no accolades or awards. No big job promotions or fancy new cars to parade around in to help me create and showboat my identity. I just had the clothes on my back and a small bin filled with my personal belongings. To add to my new image, I was riding in a police car and arriving at my destination as the newest victim of domestic violence.

SafeHomes Rape Crisis Coalition, a.k.a., welcome home.

As I checked into the facility they immediately began to dig into my past. The funny thing is that they start with questions like "what brought you in today?" Like the doctor. Well, I was abused. Is that not what your facility is for? It was really weird. It was almost if they needed to hear you admit, what caused your need their assistance. They go on to ask questions such as: How were you raised? Did you experience love as a child? Did you see your mother and father hug, kiss or hold hands? "Yes I did", I replied. "My mother and father loved each other very much". I mentioned that he passed away when I was a child.

I remember telling the interviewer there was nothing wrong with me. I just got into a bad situation, until this question: Describe your last 5 relationships. After answering almost 20 questions about myself and my past relationships with men I had the most eye opening revelation. For the exception of a few, I had dated the same man for over 10 years, they just had different names. They were all controlling, manipulative, cunning and liars. Tears drenched my face and questions flooded my mind. What caused me to be drawn to this type of man? Is this what my family could see all along? I asked myself. Tears continued to flow down my face. I'm tired of making the same mistakes God. Please help me get through this, I prayed. The intake coordinator looked at me and said, "You are strong; I can see it in you. I know you are going to make it through this." I'm glad she saw the light because all I saw around me was darkness.

We finished our hour long questionnaire session and then the intake coordinator handed me a bus pass and some referrals to local housing agencies. "Thank you for your time Ms. Hunt and good luck on your journey". I looked through the documents she had just handed me. "This is it"? I responded. Looking at what seemed to be a map and a ticket or voucher, I asked, "What is this"? "It's a bus pass and a map of the routes so you will get to your destination without getting lost", she replied with a chuckle.

I had never seen a bus pass in my life because I had not ever ridden a bus if it wasn't chartered! "All you are going to give me is a bus pass and some referrals to get help? I'm in a city where I don't know anybody." " I'm sorry Mrs. Hunt. Unfortunately, this is all the county assistance programs will allow us to give you. We have a bus we use for transportation but it's only for group outings so we will not be able to take you to work, if you get a job". This could only get better, I thought to myself. She walked me to my new room. Yes, one room, with a bathroom, a closet, four beds, 4 women, and two children. Lord, why me? The same still small voice said "Why not you? I looked around and you were the best woman for the job. I have an assignment for you to do."

The facility was very nice and quite peaceful. As I settled in I decided to take a walk on the campus down to the gazebo and get some air. Although it was a "shelter", it was very nice and upscale. I looked up to heaven and begged God to help me get through this. Just as I was wiping my tears, my phone rang. "May I speak with Brandy Hunt?" the caller asked. "This is she," I responded. The caller identified herself as the hiring manager for Disney Store, a call center I had applied to a few days prior to going to the shelter. I was hurting, not dead. Even in my ignorance I was sure that God had a plan, and if he brought me to it he would bring me through it. I remembered the scripture I was taught early on in my walk with the Lord:

"For I know the plans I have for you," declares the Lord.
Plans to prosper you and not to harm you, plans to give you a hope
and a future. Jeremiah 29:11

Thank God He had a plan because I had no idea where to start! I knew in order to care for myself or to rebuild a life for me and my daughter I would need to find some type of stable employment. I went on several interviews over the past few days but I had not heard anything back; until now.

"We would like you to start working this coming Monday. Are you available?" My heart dropped! What horrible timing I thought to myself. So much negativity exploded my mind. How will I get there? I don't have a car. It's Saturday and she wants me to start on Monday! I have two days to find transportation. I am stuck in this shelter and even though the lady gave me a bus pass the job was located outside of the bus limits. In my mind, I said no. There were too many variables. Then I heard these words, "Daughter, I am with you, take the job". "Yes! I will be there," I joyously confirmed. I was in tears by the time I hung up the phone. I was in awe at the timing of God. Did I make it to work? Of course! Not only did I get a ride to work my first day, a coworker offered to pick me up and drop me of EVERY DAY!

God is a restorer of those who diligently seek after him. You may find yourself in a similar place now. You have been dealt a hand of bad decisions and you are forced to figure out what to do. God is leading you. He has a wonderful plan. Learn to follow. You will make mistakes. You will not do everything perfect. However, all things will work together eventually if you just keep walking it out.

Unmask your face daughter. There is no shame in His Grace. The poker face is only necessary when you have something to be ashamed of. Jesus died on the cross for ALL of our sins. You can be confident in knowing you are not perfect, but we serve a perfect God! You are not here to please people, but God. How will you ever learn if you don't allow God to teach you some things? There are things that you can be taught, but there are other things you will have to live through in order to learn.

Some women showed up there with black eyes, bruised faces or body parts. They had been beaten pretty badly. I am sure they wish they had mask to cover their scars and bruises. Their scars were visible for the world to see. It was obvious they needed help. Their trauma was external. I had scars too, nobody could see them though, not even the people in church. I felt like I had been beaten. Emotionally I was drained and I had been fighting for a long time. My spirit was tired. I wanted to be a better woman than I had been. I was ready for a change.

Can You See Me Now?

Remember the Verizon commercials that showed the callers struggling with getting a cell phone signal? They would continue to move around until they had a clear signal so they could be heard on the other side. The tagline "Can you hear me now?" became one of the most popular of our generation. It wasn't the fault of the callers on either side. It was the signal, which is invisible that was causing the major problem.

So," Can you see me now"? Fear hides in our everyday lives, but if we don't know what it looks like it will continue to be entertained in our lives and control and manipulate all of our decisions. Now, fear doesn't want to be exposed or identified. Fear knows what the consequences are once it is found, immediate, instant eviction without notice. It must be put out at once! Also, keep in mind, we are not addressing actions. Actions can change depending on the situation. Your actions will change when your mindset changes. In "dealing" we are going to deal with, or in other words, address the root, so we can dig it up and it can never return again.

What exactly is Fear? And how do you deal with it once and for all so it can never return? First and foremost, there are two types of fear. The fear you have when a predator is upon you, is one type. That is not what I'm talking about. The fear I am addressing is fear that is created in the canvas of your mind. The type of fear that keeps you bound from making rational decisions for your life. It is the kind that manipulates and controls everything you do. No, it's not people controlling you, its fear.

Yes, fear is using those people to affect you. Fear is invisible. I have heard so many times fear is not real. That is not a true statement. In my experience it has been very real. However, it is not tangible. You cannot touch it but you can't touch air either. From what I know, air is real. So what is fear? Fear is a spirit. How do I know?

2 Timothy 1:7 says:
For God has not given us a spirit of fear, but of power and of love and of a sound mind.

The spirit of fear is designed to stop you from achieving your dreams and goals. Fear starts as an idea. Again, I am not talking about fear that comes from being in absolute danger. That's a natural response to help us protect ourselves. I am speaking of the type fear that binds us in an imaginary prison in our minds.

For example, I am reminded of a time that I had a loose tooth. I tried to pull it on my own, but it just would not come out. I had a thought that if I go to the dentist it's going to hurt, he will have to give me a shot and that was pain I did not want to endure. So I waited. Eventually, it became too painful to deal with and I finally got up the nerve to go to the dentist. He asked me if I wanted it pulled out that day! I didn't really, but what choice did I have? I was hurting! He numbed my gums and about two seconds later he was done! I didn't feel anything and I went back to work.

My mind had put so much fear inside of me that I did not want to feel pain even though my healing was on the other side of my pain. Do you understand this? If we can get our mind to a place where fear is not a factor we can stop begging God to heal us. Healing is available to those who are willing to endure the pain to get to the healing.

In order to deal with fear you will need to decide that fear is no longer an option. Your only option is completing the task that is before you. What would you attempt if you knew that you didn't have to be afraid to do it? Let's be honest the only reason you are afraid is because you believe you will fail.

Another reason we are fearful is because there may be pain or discomfort associated with the decision. You don't want to be seen as a failure because we rely on the approval of others. And clearly no one wants to volunteer to be humiliated or punished for our decisions. So what do you do? Just live in fear? NOOOO!! See how this can continue to be a nasty vicious cycle? Deal with the fear first. If you do, everything else will be easy.

After I ended up at the domestic violence shelter I had plenty I could be afraid of and I had a magnitude of obstacles before me. Starting over from nothing can be a fearful place you allow it, or it can be a faithful place. I decided to choose faith. There were people I hid from for months and for reasons I thought were reasonable. Yes, I was lost. Yes, I was afraid. However, it was time for me to face some hard facts. I was living in fear and I didn't know what to do about it.

The Little Engine That Shoulda

"If I were you, I would" or "You shoulda done it this way". "If you would have listened to me that would not have happened". Do those sentence starters sound familiar? They are all too familiar in my world. So many opinions on what I should do with my own life! I have yet to find the "should" list for my life. How come everybody else knows what I "should" be doing, but I barely have a clue. Better yet, why do I listen?

When people want to control your life, it will create a problem in that particular relationship. Approval addiction is rooted in fear. You always do what's on other peoples "shoulda" list for your life because you value their opinion more than your own! It never goes both ways though. When you have an opinion about their life, your advice is solicited, or welcomed.

When approval addiction dictates your decisions you are more than likely being led by emotion and not the Holy Spirit. Your fear of abandonment, or rejection, causes you to do whatever you can to keep the relationship intact. That means you probably say yes, when you want/should to say no. If you are anything like me, you paid more money than you had and stayed longer than you should have.

For a long time I was made to feel like I made so many mistakes in my lifetime that I couldn't make a good decision on my own. Years of making bad decisions led to the manipulation from men, friends, and family who made me always feel as if I was wrong. I had more confidence in the opinion of others than my own. God showed me I did not trust him. I was being obedient only AFTER I could find agreement or approval for what God told me to do. If they didn't agree, I didn't obey.

Approval addiction is also referred to as Codependency. Big word, isn't it? Some people have never even heard of the term. I know I hadn't. Expect that when you start dealing with the hand you have been dealt, that God will begin to show you some amazing things!

Codependency, by definition, means making the relationship more important to you than you are to yourself. (WebMD) Sounds crazy right! Not to a codependent personality.

In a codependent's world we stay together by any means necessary, even if the side effects of the relationship are harmful. Why? Because the fear of being alone and rejected is greater than what you have to deal with by staying in the relationship.

Most women who have been abused in anyway find themselves in codependent relationships. Like me, you may break up with one guy, but find yourself right back in another unhealthy relationship. Codependents lack boundaries. While you are "dealing" with your hand, start writing down some boundaries that you would like to have in your life. This will help show you which individual are healthy or unhealthy in your life.

Codependents are very caring people. They will literally give away what they need for themselves just to keep someone else happy or to have a false sense of peace. God has called us to be dependent in Him only. If you are depending on someone else to support you financially, physically, mentally, emotionally, or spiritually, you and that other person will eventually be bankrupt. Learn how to detach from people and their opinions of you; especially people that you have been nurturing. If you are a parent, the only people you need to nurture are your children and even that should have a time limit. People have to learn how to stand up and be responsible all on their own. You are not responsible for the wellbeing, happiness, comfort, or security of another human being to the point that it drains everything you have in you. God has given each of us our load to bear. And yes, we help each other times of need; however, you cannot give away what you don't have.

As a codependent you have to learn to say no sometimes. Yes, saying no will present a risk of rejection or abandonment, but take the risk! Let's say it's a man you want to date for example. You have a boundary set that men are not welcome to come into your home. You really like this guy and he is pressuring you to come to your house. Saying no, keeps your boundary. You set it for a reason. You have the right to remain holy! If you know that is your weakness, you may want to say no to him now, before you have to answer to God later:

Submit yourselves therefore to God, resist the devil and he will flee from you. James 4:7

Saying no means you run the risk of losing him. However, if he respects you, he will not pressure you to move past your boundary. A codependent woman will oftentimes move the boundary line and compromise just to "save face" with the gentleman. Inside she will be in turmoil about the decision she just made but she is dependent on that relationship and will do whatever it takes to keep it in tact. Sister, there are some risk that are just not worth taking.

You must decide now that regardless of how you think the outcome of a situation might be, fear will no longer be allowed to make your decisions for you. Declare with me:

I will not be afraid. Whatever God shows me is my next step, even if I am afraid of the consequences: being rejected, abandoned, and talked about, etc. I will do it unafraid. I would rather be free, than live in fear another day. He, whom the Son sets free, is free indeed. I decide on this day to live free and walk out my life in faith. Fear has had me in prison, but my Father is the prison guard, he has given me the keys to unlock my own prison. Today I free myself from the bondage that I have been held captive by for so long. I walk by faith and not by sight. I pray that God will show me where to place my boundaries and I will have enough faith not to compromise, regardless of how I feel. Regardless of who threatens to leave me, I will choose to submit to God and resist the enemy. Amen

Now that we have dealt with fear, you are a brand new person! That demonic oppression called fear can no longer hold you captive. You are free! The biggest key to dealing and staying healed is to continue to confront the spirit of fear every single time it tries to attack. Unfortunately it doesn't give up easily. But now that you know what it looks like and how to deal with it, you can stand flat footed and tell it to flee! God has not given us a spirit of fear but of love power and of a sound mind.

Remember the next time somebody offers their opinion on what you "should" do to check their motives. Are they genuinely offering sound, biblical advice or are they trying to control and manipulate your actions to benefit only themselves? Mentors are great people! We all need them, but even a great mentor lets you know this is merely advice. The choice is yours.

You know what God showed you and what God told you. God doesn't always do everything cookie cutter or normal. We serve a very creative God who may lead you to do something totally outside of the way anybody has ever done it before! Listen to the power of the Holy Spirit living inside of you. Greater is he that is in you, than he that is in the world (I John 4:4). God wants you to be able to have authority in your own life and command your own blessings. If you are always dependent on what someone else has to say or wait for them to bless you, God will not fully prosper you as he wants to. Find your "should" list in the word of God, and let people say what they will.

Dear Daughter,

Do not FEAR! I am with you. No longer will you wear a coat of shame. It's time for you to hold your head high and walk out of the pit. Get out of that dungeon. I put you in there and now I'm opening the door for you to walk out. When you get out take time to dust yourself off. Put on a new walk. Put on a new talk. Put on a new smile. You will have many opportunities. What do you want? GO FOR IT! I have placed a coat of favor on you that no man can take off of you. I'm with you always. Wherever your faith can take you, you are free to go and I'm there with you also. Hear me clearly. If you go, I will be there. And if you stay I will be there. But you have my permission to GO FORWARD! The spirit searches all things and allows you to meet up with where you should be. You are not late, you are not behind. You are being held where you are for such a time as this.

With loving kindness,

Your Father

Card # 4

Dealing with Healing

No Dealing, No Healing

Cut! Cut! Cut!

Bad Root, Bad Fruit

Know When to Fold'Em

No Dealing, No Healing

What do I do with all these cards life has handed me? I wish I could just get rid of them and start over! Why am I not able to just "get over it" and move on with my life? Or can I? This is the problem that we all face at some point in our lives. Everybody wants to "get over it" but nobody wants to deal with it. Tolerating is not the same thing as dealing. When we decide to "deal" with the cards in our hand we will soon discover that there is healing in dealing. And when you start dealing with it, you will be ridding yourself of the cards that you were once holding in your hand. When you are in relationship with Jesus Christ, he allows you to start over BRAND NEW!

And he that sat upon the throne said, Behold, I make all things new. Revelation 21:5

So, what's the difference between getting over it and dealing with it?

Let's say the kitchen floor needs to be swept. You have all the right tools; a broom, dust pan, and a trash can. You sweep the kitchen spotless. When it's time to gather the trash and brush it into the dustpan you sweep it under the rug. Did you get rid of the problem? Sure. When you walk through the kitchen you will walk "over" the rug. To the next person that comes in, your kitchen looks spotless. But you secretly know you never fully dealt with the filth. You got "over" having to look at a dirty kitchen, but you still have the issue. It's just hidden now. What we want to do is find the issue, deal with it, and get rid of all evidence so that when the next person comes in they don't kick the rug and have the entire mess be exposed from under it. This will ultimately leave you feeling ashamed and embarrassed.

So how do you "deal" with ALL these issues? The main thing will be TRUTH.

And you will know the truth, and the truth will make you free. John 8:32

You have to be honest with God, yourself, and others. At first, this will not be an easy task. But you cannot be fearful of the outcome. However, being honest about who you are and where you are will get you a lot further than trying to sugar coat your issue. I cannot tell you how to act in every situation that is presented in your lifetime. There are way too many scenarios to conquer in one book. Heck, I may not be able to address all your individual issues in one lifetime!

This is what I can do: I can help you realize the truth about who you are. The person God created for you to be, regardless of culture, age, race, shortcomings, or disappointments. For example, if you are dealing with abandonment what you are feeling is lonely, also, maybe inadequate, unloved, and betrayed. Those are all feelings and may come and go at any time. The truth is: You are chosen, a royal priesthood, a holy nation.

But you are a chosen generation, a royal priesthood, a holy nation, His owns special people, that you may proclaim the praises of Him who called you out of darkness into His marvelous light.
I Peter 2:9

The bible is full of God's true love for us. We must take time to sit with him and find out how much he really loves us, and desires to be our Father.

As I stared into the mirror questions began to flood my mind. I was looking into a mirror at myself. The image had not changed, but I wasn't confident about who was staring back at me. I sure didn't feel chosen. What happened to me? Where was the real me? Why did I let this happen? What should I have done differently?

I looked in the mirror and was not happy about who was looking back at me, at all. I wanted to be a better woman than I had become. I thought back to the conversation I had with the intake counselor. In order to heal, I would have to deal with the issues I had ignored for years.

Interrupting my negativity, I heard the Holy Spirit speak these words "I'm going to remove the mask. First, I am eliminating everything and everybody that does not bring glory to My name." There you go again, God, with these warnings that don't make sense, I thought to myself. While I'm sure He knew exactly what He meant, I on the other hand was quite baffled. "How?" I asked. "First, get rid of all the wigs you own and do not put anymore weave in your hair." If I could tweet my response to God my hash tag would looked something like this:

#OHNOYOUDIDN'!!!

WHAAAAAT! Oh no God. You don't mess with a woman's hair! Besides, He had already taken everything else. Now you want to take my hair too? "Seriously God, why my hair"? I questioned.

From the time I was very young, maybe 14, I was very good at doing hair. I had different hair styles on a regular basis. It was somewhat of a creative outlet for me. People would give me compliment after compliment over how good of a job I did and how pretty it was. God showed me that over the years I started doing it to only fuel my approval addiction. My self-worth was so low; I needed to feed off of the approval of other people, which I wore with pride and honor. It gave me a sense of accomplishment, beauty, and acceptance.

Wow! Really God? I didn't see it that way. That was probably because I had done it so long it had become second nature to me. So he got rid of it. It didn't make sense then, but it totally makes sense now. As I stated before you have to deal with issues from the root.

"It's time for you to go natural." This was only an external explanation of what God was doing to me internally.

Right now? No transition? Let me ease my way into it! I mean I considered going natural, but what would people think? What if it's ugly! Uh, no thank you God. How about I just curl my real hair, no weave? I am quite sure you never compromise with God, but I do. At least I try to anyway. Reluctant about this "natural" thing, I went to the beauty supply store in search of an alternative method. After struggling with God, and God not budging, I agreed to get rid of my "hair collection" and just wear my regular hair. However, the "big chop" was out of the question.

For those of you who may not be familiar with natural hair terms, let me explain. The "big chop" is when you cut all of your hair off that has been chemically processed. For me that meant relaxed parts which was equivalent to about 10 inches of hair! I would only have about an inch of hair left. I was terrified.

As I walked up and down the isle of the beauty supply store deciding if I wanted a relaxer or some hair color God reminded me of what he said. "Brandy, Go natural". I said ok God, if you want me to go natural send somebody in this store to tell me to do so as I continued my exploration of hair products. While standing in the isle between relaxers and hair color a lady walked up next to me wearing a hat. We began some small talk and she asked me what I was looking for and I replied, "I was trying to decide if I'm going natural, getting a relaxer, or color." She took off her hat and said, "It's the best thing I have done to my hair. I'm natural and I love it. Go for it! You won't regret it," she exclaimed with a smile. At that very moment, my struggle with God ended.

Why? Because the God of the universe doesn't owe me a thing, yet he decided to care enough about me to send me a sign. I surrendered my heart to the Lord. And at that moment the cutting began.

I stood in my mirror at a domestic violence shelter in the back woods of nowhere, and cut my shoulder length hair, from tip to root. Cutting away all the negativity I had been through, cutting away all the pain and anger and cutting away all the bitterness and hatred that had burdened me for so long. Not just from the break up, I mean everything. It was actually quite refreshing. I was being allowed the chance to start fresh.

As I was cutting I was remembering all the negative things I heard about wanting to go natural. My ex-husband begged me not to go natural. He didn't think it would "fit" me. I even had several friends tell me that I would hate it. I had many more excuses of my own, but when God tells you to do something and then confirms it Himself, it would be best if you obey Him. I began to imagine what people were going to say. "Why did you do that?"

I knew I would be too ashamed to say because God told me to, and I wasn't bold enough to say because I felt like it! I also wondered if men still be attracted to me? Will my family like it? Will anybody like it for that matter? Will I like it? God interrupted my thought pattern. How would I know? I never get a chance to have an opinion. I try to avoid conflict at all cost, so I just do what others want me to. It just makes things easier. I didn't even want the conflict that would arise out of even having made a decision about my OWN hair!

When you first decide to deal with the issues that have haunted your past, nobody will be there but you. Yes, physically there may be people around you, but this is between you and God. As a matter of fact, when you begin to walk in the truth of who you really are, you may not find many people agree with you, but that's ok, be you anyway. You fought your whole life defending everybody else. Isn't it time you defend yourself? You don't have to receive the approval of men to be obedient to God.

I love people. I love to be around groups of people, hang out and have fun. But the reality is that, there is a time for everything and when you are in a season of regrouping, it is a time to be alone. You need to get away from the noise, business of life and the opinions and expectations others. You need time to just get away, sit with God and reflect. Sticking yourself in a room and crying your eyes out about how horrible you think you are, because of what you have done, is not how God wishes for you to deal with it. That is called condemnation. However, make time to get alone to worship and praise God. He will show you His plan, and He will show it to you as soon as you can get away from the noise.

While you are away and reflecting don't allow the destroyer to pile up your problems and stack them against you.

Yes, you have made some bad decisions in your lifetime. However, there is nothing you have done that catches God by surprise. You are forgiven.

Satan condemns God convicts.

Condemnation is to express strong disapproval of or blame. Conviction is a firmly held belief. In other words condemnation points the finger and says you did it, now you will have to pay the price.

There is therefore now no condemnation to them which are in Christ Jesus, who walk not after the flesh but after the Spirit. For the law of the Spirit of life in Christ Jesus hath made me free from the law of sin and death. Roman: 8:1

God says yes, I know you did it, now how can I help you change so you don't do it again? It is not brash or harsh. It can sometimes be as simple as God nudging you to apologize for something you did or said to somebody. God had already decided to forgive you before you did it. The condemnation of the evil one however, will bring condemning thoughts and demand you be sent to hell for what you have done. It's that feeling of guilt that we can never seem to shake. However, because of the sacrifice Jesus Christ made on the cross, when we are in Him we can be assured that He has already paid the price for our sin and we don't have to be condemned for every wrong action we make. This is one of the benefits of salvation. Have you accepted Christ as your personal savior yet? There is a prayer in the back of the book to lead you to salvation.

The ultimate key to *"Dealing with the Hand You Were Dealt"* is willingness. No matter the issue, we must be willing to address it, so we can get free from whatever is holding us in bondage. You will never be able to deal with what you are not willing to confront. Remember, no fear right? Yes, you are going to cry, don't be afraid. Yes, people will leave you, do not be afraid. Yes, you will have to walk alone. But it's ok. Be of good courage.

Be brave, be strong. Don't give up. Expect God to get here soon. Psalm 31:24

To deal with the truth you must first deal with its opposite. Yes, lie is the opposite of truth, but the reason why we lie is FEAR! Fear is the reason many of us don't move from where we are to where we want to go. A lot of people get stuck here. They look at what they have gone through or all that they have endured and use it to calculate their outcome. It's a very dangerous place to be.

Look at dealing this way; if you decide to cut down, de-root and remove an entire tree, including the stump, you will need to uproot it. But first you must chop down the tree, then chop the stump and ultimately deal with the root. Fear is at the root of ALL situations where there is conflict. However, God may start dealing with you in an entirely different area. Be patient, he is working his way to the root of your issue. Be willing and be obedient.

Somebody reading this book is afraid of what the end result will be. The shame that you carry because of your past is wiped away at this very moment. You can lift your head. You cannot be afraid of what might happen to you or what your family and friends may think of you. Fear of conflict is one of the deceiver's biggest lies. God has promised to be our protector. It's time to deal with the truth. Make up in your mind that regardless if you are alone after this process is over or you have a million people supporting you, there is no more fear. Fear no longer has a say so in the matters of the heart, mind, body, soul, or spirit.

In order to get to the root and the truth, you have to expose all lies. To get through this process to the truth you have to be willing to embrace the pain of your decisions. Those are very hurtful places that you are about to visit. Believe me when I say if you remove the fear, everything else is easy.

Even as I wrote this book, I had to revisit some very painful experiences. My primary issue, the root of my pain, was the death of my father. As I go to work every day I pass the church and graveside where my Father's funeral was held. I have refused to go there for years, probably at least 15. I didn't want to face it. First of all, I was afraid of going to a graveyard. Secondly, I knew he wasn't there. His body might be, but it surely had decayed by now. God spoke to me and told me to go to the gravesite. As I drove silently upon the graveyard, fearful but at peace, I knew God was there. I slowly exited the car. As it had been 15 years I didn't even know where the tomb was located. As I walked and walked and walked, I became angry and a little frustrated. I cried aloud, "Why, God, why am I here if I can't even find it?" I got into my car with tears of frustration streaming down my face and drove off hysterically. "Oh well. I went so I'm done", I whimpered. "Not so fast daughter. Go back tomorrow."

See, we do this a lot in our lives. We pretend because we touched on the surface that we actually dealt with it. As my normal route takes me takes me by there every day, I ventured to go home and as I was passing the gravesite, God nudged me to go again. This time, I was certain I would find it. I refused to leave until I did. I stood among the tombs and looked around. I closed my eyes and went back to the day we walked upon the graveside to say our final respects. The day I watched him lowered into the ground. I saw it as clear as day. I then began to walk the path I walked that day, and I walked straight to the spot where I left him. I screamed out loud.

Daddy! Why did you leave me here to face this world all alone! Didn't you know I needed you daddy? I miss you sooo much! I know if you were here you would be so proud of us. We miss you dearly. I know you have been with me throughout my days. I have a daughter, Aniya. You have the most precious grandchildren in the world. We still fight, that hasn't changed! But we love each other and we stick together like you taught us. Mom does a great job taking care of us, AND everybody else. Yes, she still takes on way too much cause she wants to help everybody. Dad, I forgive you. I blamed you for the things I have been through, but I was wrong. It was not your fault. I had to go through it. I am sorry for ever doubting Gods plan for my life, and your life. Your life was not your own, and neither is mine. We are all here to serve a purpose, and once the purpose is done, so is our journey. Thank you for the time you spent with me on your journey. I love you Daddy.

I opened my eyes to realize I was now kneeling and my tears had watered his grave. I was not afraid anymore and I was at peace; the peace the Bible talks about that passes all understanding.

Numerous times God has shown me he is a healer and a comforter. I promise He will be with you as well.

Pray this prayer aloud:

Here I am Lord; show me the truth ABOUT ME. Help me deal with me. If it hurts, comfort me; if it causes me to have to walk alone, be a friend to me; and if it causes radical change, be my courage in the face of all my fears.

In Jesus Name,
Amen

This is not a common way to start a prayer because our generation wants to blame everything on everybody else. This was my prayer as I woke up every day in a foreign place with strangers. I didn't have my child, my husband, my family, my car, my belongings and I only had a few people I could really call friend. I knew once I dealt with the painful reality of the past, God would give me back all that I lost. Regrettably for now, I was miserable, heartbroken, bitter, anguished, afraid and lonely. I was messed up!

I remember standing in the mirror saying these words. "Who Am I?" I answered before God could have time to respond. I'm ugly. I'm fat. Nobody is ever going to love me again. I'm never going to recover from this. I'm stupid. I made the biggest mistake of my life. Just as I had I began to flood my room with negativity, God stopped me. "You are Victoria," I heard a voice inside me whisper. What? Who is Victoria? My name is Brandy. Maybe I am hearing things, I thought to myself. The Holy Spirit whispered "find out the meaning and that's who you are, no matter what you see or how you feel. Don't let anybody tell you any different." I was confused, so I asked one of the girls on campus. Her name just happened to be Victoria, so I figured she would know what it meant. She informed me that the name Victoria derived from the male name, Victor, and in Spanish it meant, Victory! I did some more research and discovered that in Latin in meant conqueror and English its definition was triumphant!

Wow God! Really? In my greatest day of defeat you choose to call me victorious! I am triumphant? If I didn't think God was crazy and weird before now, I really thought it at this moment. God have you taken a look at my shattered life and as I wallowed still in defeat a scripture captivated my heart: God reminded me of His word. "I told you in Romans 4:17 to speak those things that are not, as though they were. Why would I not do the same thing? I called you to be before the foundation of this earth and you ARE victorious! From now on act like it and don't let another day go by that you are down, depressed or unhappy. I told you I am with you and this is not about you. I have an assignment for you to complete."

I finished the "big chop" on my hair confident that from that day on my life had changed the moment my name changed and I would never be the same again.

Cut! Cut! Cut!

They say the truth hurts, but life has taught me so does lies. God had been cutting into my life in so many ways. I was honestly ready for him to stop. But the cutting is necessary if the issue is deep. It helps you get down to the issue, quickly and swiftly. Just like a surgeon. If a surgeon came in with a fork to operate, he is not going to get too far is he? He will need to use the proper tool that is effective in getting through the tough outer surface so that he can address the issue. Such is life.

As I write this chapter I am currently recovering from major surgery. Really God? This has to happen right in the middle of a major milestone? I don't have time for setbacks or delays. But this time I wasn't backing down and I wasn't quitting from what I had set my mind to do. I tried to avoid surgery at all cost. There are some people who adapt to surgery and a hospital like it's nothing. I am not one of those people. I wanted God to supernaturally heal me.

When I was about 23 years old I was diagnosed with fibroid tumors. At the time, 10 years ago, there were only 2, though they caused me enormous pain. Most women either have them or will have them at some point in their lives. Doctors say they don't know where they come from, or how to get rid of them. Had I known sooner that there were natural methods to heal myself from them; I may have been able to try them. I did try several of the doctor's options, but to no avail. Nothing worked. Over the years I left them untreated. The pain eventually left, but the issue was still there. What little pain and symptoms I had, I grew accustomed to so I ignored it. However, my other internal organs were suffering greatly.

The fibroids had increased in number from 2 to 7. The size of my uterus was half the size of a basketball! I was beginning to look pregnant, feel pregnant and act pregnant! I'm talking hormone fits and hunger cravings! I was even once asked when my baby was due. My spine had shifted to make room for the enlarged uterus. The point is that if you leave something unresolved long enough, it will eventually begin to affect everything that surrounds it. Even if there is no pain, it doesn't mean that the problem is gone.

I saw doctor after doctor, at least 5 and they all suggested a hysterectomy; though my age was considered as they didn't want to take away my option to have more children. I prayed about it for a while and tried to use wisdom in making my decision. It had been 10 years that I had trusted God to supernaturally heal me. I wasn't expecting to get married anytime soon, and my daughter is now 13. I really don't expect to have any more children and I am ok with that! I have grown to love children and I would adopt if I had the opportunity. I know what abandonment feels like and I would love the opportunity to give love to a child who feels helpless and hopeless. So that objective was quickly over ruled. The one objective they could not overcome was that they would have to cut me open as if I were having c-section. Oh my God! Do you know what drastic measures you have to go through to heal from that type of cut? I had heard about several procedures where they would not have to cut me, but I was not eligible for those.

Really, I was not surprised. I always get the hard road, in my opinion. I suppose it is God's way of making me strong. How can I suggest you deal with your life, and be unwilling to deal with my own? Yes, I was afraid. I thought of all the things that could go wrong. I could die on the operating table. What if I become paralyzed from the Dr. hitting a vein or artery during surgery? So many negative thoughts flooded my mind at one time! "No!" I declared to Satan and all his evil forces. "I AM HEALED. I SHALL LIVE AND NOT DIE TO DECLARE THE WORKS OF THE LORD."

I scheduled my surgery and I put my fears and worries aside, and this time I didn't back down. I knew the cut would be painful. Not just the day of, but I was informed that a few months later, I would still feel pain. I also knew that the cut would ultimately leave a visible scar that would be ugly for the rest of my life. I decided that it's my scar and it is proof that I survived the big CUT! It was proof that the issue had been dealt with and all I had to deal with was a scar. Well to God be the Glory! So sister if you have emotional or physical scars, that only shows that you survived the battle! Those marks are not ugly, but beautiful in His sight.

The day I woke up from surgery was a marvelous day. I knew that I had made it through a 10 year battle within and now I was FREE from pain. Yes, I had pain from the cut, but fibroids would no longer be able to affect me. My hormones would be back to normal and I wouldn't be the raging hormonal beast that I had once been.

The next day after my surgery a fever struck my body! The doctors were baffled as they could not find any infection in my body. They could not identify the infected area, but they still treated me. I was not surprised. Conflict always comes to test us but this time I knew it wasn't going to stop me! I knew God; my heavenly Father was keeping me there for a reason. Even if I did not know what it was at that particular moment -sometime we have to free our minds from needing to know everything. God knew there was still something that needed to be dealt with and he wouldn't let me take it back home with me. I was just thankful I was going home a brand new person! One of the goals from the nurses in the hospital was for me to walk every day. I wanted to ask them, "You do know I have a 5 inch long cut on my stomach right?" This was soooo hard for me. It seemed to take every bit of energy I had to push forward. I could barely breathe, and they wanted me to walk too? Nevertheless, I was determined to not let this get the best of me. I knew I was healed because that's what I came there for! The doctor had done his part, now it was time for me to do mine.

I walked the halls of the hospital singing worship songs and declaring my healing. While they were looking for the infected area I was declaring my healing. They poked and prodded me at least 15-20 times with needles and IV's. I was so ready to go home. Finally, 7 days after my surgery I left the hospital. Seven is the number of completion. God once again confirmed himself to me that my season of pain was over. He had made the necessary CUT that I needed in my life to deal with my issues. It was deep, it was painful, and now it was OVER!

Emotional cutting is somewhat like a physical cut. In dealing with the hand you were dealt, you will be cut. DEEP. With what? Mainly the tool God will use to cut is truth. This truth may be revealing a certain person is no good for you and why you need to cut them out of your life. You can try to get around it as much as you like, but you will eventually have to have a face-off with the truth. Dealing with the truth when it comes to God is all about allowing him to cut down to the deep places. About what? You. When it is all said and done you know your own story. Are you really portraying the role of a Woman of God? The daughter of the King? Are you walking out into your purpose and destiny according to the script God showed you? Have you snuck off and added your own characters to the scene? Have you created relationships where your role called for you to be alone? Are you wearing the "poker face" or are you being real? You know who you are and why you hide from God and others. You know your deepest fears and you greatest accomplishments. Your fear of dealing with the truth is rooted in abandonment and rejection. If anyone were to find out who you really are would they see the real you? Therefore, your greatest fear is losing them. So ultimately you pretend to be who they think you are instead of being who you really are.

Now after the cut, you must go through recovery. I thought this would be a time where friends and family would fill my home with good food, gifts, and visits. In the first few days that is exactly what happened. I was amazed at the outpouring of love I was shown. And then I was left to deal with, me, all alone in my house. The feelings of rejection that I faced were sometimes unreal! I felt unloved. I felt as if no one cared about me. Days went by without even a phone call. I cried out to God and asked why he would let something like this happen. He responded very sweetly, "You have to be alright with walking alone sometimes." I had to remind myself that the people calling me or stopping by didn't confirm or deny my ability to be loved. I was already loved! I wasn't abandoned. God was right there with me. I began to appreciate the alone time, and the quiet space that God had blessed me with. Ultimately, after I was fully healed I could see a difference not just in my physical appearance, but also my emotional. I lost about 15 pounds in the physical, let the church say: AMEN! But I dropped even more weight in the spirit. My emotional weight had been lifted! I felt so light. God had removed my burdens and gave me peace. I learned that one must expect that there will be a purpose in your pain.

CUT! This is a word used by every director that has been in charge of television, movies, commercials and stage plays. If a director calls CUT! Houston, we may have a problem. Picture this: The scene is set and you have reviewed the script a thousand times. You know your lines and your scene partner's lines as well. You have it memorized and could repeat it in your sleep. "And Action!" All of a sudden your scene partner begins to act out a scene from a totally different movie because he wanted to. He liked it better. What are you going to do now? Your lines don't match what he is doing but before he can get any further you will hear these words:

Cut! Cut! Cut! The director cannot allow this to continue on as is. The script was written so that he can display a particular truth through a character. Right now this actor is not portraying who he needs him to be. Isn't this like life? God has written our story to play out a particular way and he is yelling Cut! We are acting out the story how we want it to be and not the way he showed it to us. We know how we should act as children of the King, but instead we act as if we have no home training, as my grandma used to say. We are running around fighting each other instead of loving one another because we barely love ourselves. God has made us promises for our lives and written them in the script but because we have veered off to do our own thing and create our own role we will never get what God intends for us to have. Thankfully, God loves us enough to call CUT, in our lives.

Now after the director calls cut, there is a small meeting of the minds. The script is reviewed to find out where the fault lies. Meaning, where did we mess up? When did the actor get off script? Let's rewind and start there. This is what we have to do sometimes. Go back to the place where it all began. For some it was the day your father left. For others it may be your mother, siblings, or friends. There are people who hold old jobs responsible for their lack of skill. There are all kinds of issues that people deal with. Regardless of your issue, check your reel and go back to the place where it got off track.

AND....ACTION!

Bad Root, Bad Fruit

Even so, every good tree bears good fruit, but a bad tree bears bad fruit. A good tree cannot bear bad fruit, nor can a bad tree bear good fruit. Every tree that does not bear good fruit is cut down and thrown into the fire. Therefore by their fruits you will know them.

Matthew 7:17-20

Guess what? After you deal with the truth of how you got here, it's time to deal with how you will move forward. Isn't that your goal? Healing, Wholeness, and Forgiveness. This is a must. Period. You can do the 12 steps to recovery program but if this isn't one of them you might as well not do them at all. If I stress any one topic other than fear it will be this one. If you don t take anything else away from this book take this one truth: Forgive, Whomever, for whatever.

Matthew 6:14
For if you forgive men their trespasses, your heavenly father will also forgive you.

Forgiveness is simply this: the inner ability to free someone from any penalty they would receive from what they did to you. There is a reward not only for them, but for you. As you continue to forgive, you are forgiven. Yes, you are releasing yourself and them, from the prison of their past mistakes that you put them in. Do they deserve to be punished? Probably, but let God handle their punishment. Your heart can only carry so much weight.

Throughout this lifetime we go through so many difficult trials and test that we begin to build resentment and hate towards certain people and certain relationships. I have given you a brief explanation of some of the things I have gone through in my lifetime. You may have gone through similar or worse situations.

I know what they did to you was horrible. However, the fact remains that you must forgive. I know what you are saying; you don't know what they did to me or they deserve to be punished. You are absolutely right. I don't know what they did, but it doesn't matter. You may or may not face the person who wronged you again. I did and I am so glad I had already dealt with it.

While I was finishing my last year of high school, I was a waitress at a major food corporation. The supervisor had agreed to let us wear tennis skirts because the AC was broken, so he said. We thought nothing of it, until one day as I was leaving for work my supervisor called me into his office to discuss a guest complaint. "Brandy, I need to see you in my office after closing." "Why? What did I do?" I mumbled under my breath. "Ok", I replied. Up then I had been a rather good employee, so I thought nothing of it.

A few minutes after closing, I stood in the back office waiting to hear what the complaining guest had to say. Instead I was presented with these words. "I see how you have been looking at me". Just then he began to walk towards me. I began to try to run out the door. Unfortunately, this office had one way in and one way out, through the same door. He pressed l his genital area up against me. I screamed. "No! Please don't let this happen again!" I pushed him but he resisted. "Stop!" I screamed. I then kicked him in the groin and ran out the back door as my mom pulled up. I got in the car and explained what happened and she told me to quit my job. I never went back. In my mind I thought. That's it? Aren't we fighting back? My mom wasn't a fighter; she would just rather walk away and be done with it. So I did what she said and I carried that experience with me for years. As, he was also a bouncer at some of the clubs around the city, I would seen him and be terrified to be in his presence.

As I went through my healing process, I decided it was time to forgive him as well. Even though he didn't rape me, his attempt to defame my character and treat me as some low class prostitute still stuck with me 10 years later. I decided to forgive him and move on with my life. I was sure he had.

So here we are, as I started out, you never know who you will run into again right? My grandmother passed away while I was living in Atlanta and I drove back home to attend the funeral. As I walked through the front door to greet my family at the funeral home, the funeral directors entered after me, and as we were receiving instructions, I heard an old but familiar voice. I froze in my tracks. I slowly turned around and staring me in my face was the man that had assaulted me 10 years earlier. He was all smiles for the grieving family. I felt like screaming! Get out you molester! I wanted to tell my mom, remember when I was molested at work? Don't talk to him! That was 10 years ago and just as God had forgiven me, I had to forgive him. He will never know that he put years of pain inside of me. This is probably not the appropriate moment to tell him either. I forgave him. Not for formality, or the thing to do, but for real and so that I could be free. By forgiving him, I was able to accept him consoling me and my family and he even drove me to my grandmother's funeral. Isn't it funny how life turns things around?

Forgiveness is not for the other person. It is for you. I may not get the chance to physically connect with everybody that has ever wronged me, but it's ok. I have forgiven them and made peace with them in my heart and that's all that matters. Reconciliation is possible but not always necessary.

Many times in the Bible God asks us to forgive. I am reminded of the story of Jesus on the cross. After he had been beaten, whipped and was hanging from a cross he uttered these words, "Father, forgive them, for they know not what they do". Our savior is dying for our sins and yet at the same time asking that we be forgiven for hanging him on the cross. What an awesome example of forgiveness for us to follow.

Dealing with forgiveness is a constant battle of the need to be right. Forgiving doesn't mean that the other person was right and you were wrong. It means you know they were wrong but you have decided in your heart that their wrong is not strong enough to dictate how you make your decisions in your life. You are still who you are regardless of what they did to you. God will never attach your identity to something external or tangible. You are not your experiences.

Check the fruit on your tree. Bad root will produce a bad fruit. The life of the fruit did not begin when the fruit began to grow on the tree. The life of the fruit began with the seed was planted. The apple tree will continue to grow apples from the one seed that was planted forever and always. It will never grow oranges. However, there is no guarantee the fruit of the tree is going to be healthy unless you take care of the root of the tree. If you don't take care of the root, if an apple grows rotten on a tree it's too late. You must throw it away. However, if you want healthy fruit you water the root, till the soil and make sure that it gets light. Such is life; if the fruit of your life is negative check what is at the root. Are you watering your life with the word of God or everything worldly that you can seem to find? Are you tilling the soil and keeping out the weeds? Are you keeping out negative thoughts, people, and ideas? And lastly, is your life showing enough light? Are you participating in darkness with the evil one?

If there is bad fruit, it's okay to let it die and fall to the ground. The good thing is that the seed in the apple can still be of some use, another year will come around for your tree to potentially grow new apples. Check your roots. You deserve to have good fruit in your life. God has given you everything you need to do so. Have you forgiven everybody that has ever done you wrong? Be sure to include God and yourself.

Once you have dug up the nasty roots of your past and exposed the lies, hatred, bitterness and resentment, next you need to replace it with something fruitful. That which you have removed is unfruitful and will never have anything good to grow from it. In Galatians 5, we are actually given 9 fruits of the spirit. Why not put something in its place that is everlasting and eternal, always abounding in sacrifice and commitment, unconditional, unconventional, and sometimes overwhelming? What will go in its place? The nine fruits of the spirit are: love, joy, peace, patience, kindness, goodness, faithfulness, gentleness, and self-control.

You might as well not even try to deal with forgiveness if you cannot choose to love in spite of how you feel. Of all the fruits we have received, it seems as if love is the hardest to comprehend. Love is a very complex, yet simple, non-emotional, yet intangible experience. It is one of the most sought after experiences on this earth. People steal, kill, and destroy over it. You may have even found yourself in a situation or two fighting in the name of love. Love is a decision. It is an inner commitment to remain constant and compassionate with another human being or creation, without condition. What's so hard about that? To be constant, compassionate, and committed, that's the easy part. The hard part is unconditional. That means that we don't wait until somebody gets it all "right" to forgive. We don't wait until they do what we want them to do, to lend a helping hand. No we are not doormats, so never be the one doing everything, but always be willing to go first. God sees your heart, and he knows your motive and your intentions.

Know When to Fold'Em

Have you ever heard of the expression, "know when to hold'em and when to fold'em"? In the game of Poker, to hold'em means to stay with the cards you've got and to fold'em means to throw in your hand and withdraw from the game being played. Basically, a player has ultimately decided, judging by the cards they have been dealt, that their chances of winning are slim to none. Thus, the player that has decided to "fold" has decided to throw in his losing hand and the player that has decided to hold has decided that the cards in his hand are potential winners.

This is how we act when dealing with forgiveness. But we have it backwards. We are holding the losing cards and we are folding on the winning cards! So many times we walk around having made a decision to hold'em. We hold on to pain, as if it is our friend. We hold on to bitterness and anger, like a new pair of shoes. Regrettably, our win is really a loss; especially when we may have won the argument, with our spouse, significant other or family member! We fought for the right to be right, and we won, but we lost the relationship. What should have mattered to us the most? In essence, we hold on to things we should have let go of a long time ago and let go of things that are worth holding on to.

As we have gone through the specifics of life and the circumstances, I have not only picked up the tragedy that happened but I have also picked up the cards of what it left behind. I was mad at the people that did it to me, God and me.

I had carried unforgivingness with me for so long that it had become a part of who I was. Anger was a normal emotion for me, and happiness was reserved for holidays and family gatherings. I walked around angry and with a chip on my shoulder for the guilty and the not guilty. The resentment that I had for the people around me was astronomical. I had been rejected by so many people that I truly believed I was not wanted and started to treat others the same.

It is true, hurting people hurt other people. It's a vicious cycle that only changes when we decide to. Many people ask, "Well, how can you just forgive somebody who hurt you so badly"? You just do it. I didn't want to play games with God anymore. I was hurting so badly and I was ready to surrender to do things the right way. His way.

He began to lead me to several scriptures that helped me to stop holding and start folding. I had to stop holding incidences and experiences against other people. I had to walk away from toxic people that meant me no good. I had to fold and surrender to love. I had to let God love me, even when I didn't want him to because I didn't believe I deserved it. God is love. Love is what you must ultimately give yourself over to so that you can be fully healed. You are not condoning of what they did to you but God says that the battle belongs to Him; the walk of love belongs to us. Not being able to forgive those who hurt you will never give you a winning hand. It is poison to your soul and a loser's hand. If it is not dealt with it will flow over into other areas of your life and your life will become a disaster if it's not already.

I believe in marriage. I believe God is able to heal and prosper a marriage that is on the verge of divorce. I believe in the unbreakable bond between two people. My grandparents celebrated 50 years of marriage a month before my grandmother passed away. I saw them press through difficult times and triumph. Heartbreakingly enough, I would not be fortunate enough to walk in their shoes.

I had a bit of a different story. I love the simplicity of the lyrics by Kenny Rogers. It simply tells us:

He said, "If you're gonna play the game, boy
You gotta learn to play it right

You've got to know when to hold 'em
Know when to fold 'em
Know when to walk away
Know when to run
You never count your money
When you're sittin' at the table
There'll be time enough for countin'
When the dealin's done

Every gambler knows

That the secret to survivin'
Is knowin' what to throw away
And knowin' what to keep

I decided to fold'em as I couldn't do it anymore. I had held it together so long and I had tried hard. Yes, I had even spoken to my husband a few weeks after I had been in the domestic violence shelter. As usual, he was talking the same, he wasn't changing but I had totally changed! I was no longer afraid of how he was going to feel about my response.

I offered him reconciliation under two conditions: 1) He would have to date me again, as we prepared to remarry; and 2) he would have to provide somewhere for me and my daughter to live before we could get back together. He was beside himself. "What! Date my wife? I'm not doing that. You just need to come back to me." "And to what?" I asked, "We don't have anything. You and I are both homeless. All I am asking is that you show me you can provide for me and my daughter. At least try." Remember, I had been the man, the provider, and the head of the family, in the relationship for so long. I had provided everything - money, resources, spiritual support. I was tired!! I was merely asking to switch seats. I wanted God's order for my life. This would also prove if God was in this relationship. I wholeheartedly believe, when God gives a vision he will provide provision. The reason I asked about dating again was because he had said we were only together because of the marriage license. Therefore, I wanted him to prove his love for me! I even told him that I was open to counseling before we lived together again. I TRIED! He would not budge. No, was no. Obviously, God is not in it and I folded.

When the divorce attorney came by the shelter to offer free service to victims of domestic violence, I signed the necessary paperwork and started the order of separation. You want to talk about a gut wrenching experience? I never in my wildest dreams would have thought my life would end up with a testimony of divorce and domestic violence. At this point, I lifted my hands and surrendered to the process and thought, God, my life is your hands. Do with it what you will. God showed me a verse that again reminded me that He was with me;

*"Fear not, for you will not be put to shame and do not feel
humiliated, for you will not be disgraced; but you will forget
the shame of your youth, and the reproach of your widowhood
you will remember no more. For your husband is your Maker,
whose name is the Lord of hosts; and your Redeemer is the
Holy One of Israel, who is called the God of all the earth. For
the lord has called you, like a wife forsaken and grieved in
spirit, even like a wife of one's youth when she is rejected,"
says your God. "For a brief moment I forsook you, but with
great compassion I will gather you. In an outburst of anger I
hid my face for a moment, but with everlasting loving-kindness
I will have compassion on you," says the Lord your Redeemer.
Isaiah 54:4-8*

There is something about knowing that even though my
earthly father is gone, and my earthly husband has forsaken and
rejected me, that God still cares! He is both my husband and my
Father. This is what fuels me to live a better life.

I don't know what kind of relationship you have had with
your father, or with men in general. If it has been a rocky road
please believe me, if you trust in God he can make your path
crystal clear. Let go of trying to piece together happiness. Let go
of trying to keep a man just so you won't be alone. I know there is
someone reading this right now that is only in a relationship
because they want to be loved. Ultimately, you will end up alone
anyway.

It's not your fault, we were born to love. But it's time to let
him go. In the future, ask God to show you who should and should
not give your love to. Ask God to help you take your time before
giving yourself away. This may be giving of self, time, money,
resources, and of course sex. There is nothing wrong with you for
doing so, as you will learn; it's in our nature to be givers, nurturers,
and lovers. Regrettably, when you are "fatherless" many times you
end up being the one who is hurt, broke and alone.

Trust your heavenly Father even if he says "no, he's not the
one". Submission, order, and discipline are a few of the things that
we may have missed out on as little girls. We are not accustomed

to a man telling us what to do. Couples who marry often find themselves in disagreements because the wife won't "submit" to her husband. Well, if she is a fatherless daughter she is not used to a man guiding her. If she has been raped she may have a fear of being controlled. Being fatherless makes you very fragile; therefore, be careful who you allow to care for you. Make sure they have a full understanding of who you really are. Prayerfully, they will be supportive of your healing. Being fatherless is an experience, and though it may last a long time, it is not a life sentence. God made sure he covered you in that area. He is your Father.

Also, remember, though life did deal you this hand, YOU get to choose its title. Don't let the label of divorce, single mom, widow, or fatherless be your title. Ask God to give you a new name. He will wipe your slate clean that you need never be ashamed of your past.

Dear Daughter,

I have not given you a spirit of fear, but of power, love, and a sound mind. Pray for a spirit of boldness in this season. You will need it for the territories and cities I am taking you in. Declare what I have spoken to you with accuracy and clarity. Do not be afraid for I Am with you. You have not spent one day alone. Take time for yourself. Not you and a friend. Just you. Anything. It's okay to be alone. The word "ONE" is at the center of aloneness. Without sitting alone with yourself, your "one", you will never be any good to join together as "two". Everything is going to be alright. All things work together. I will use every bad day and every good day to work out for your good. I called you from the foundations of the world knowing all that you would endure. Nothing you have been through will ever be wasted. I will use all things for your good, and My Glory! Don't drag your feet in being obedient to my word. Think past your current circumstance. This is only temporary.

Endless Love,

Your Father

Card # 5

Dealing with Destiny

Show Me the W.A.I.

Lights! Camera! Action!

Free At Last

Show Me the W.A.I.

"Hello sir I am lost, Can you show me the W.A.I? Not the WAY as most are accustomed to as in directional, but W.A.I. Who Am I? Where Am I? Why Am I here? Where Am I going? I NEED MY IDENTITY!" These are what I conclude are the unwritten and unspoken words of Eve at the beginning of woman's' existence. I am very convinced that these were a few of the first questions on Eve's mind when she arrived in the Garden of Eden. Even today, it is every woman's deepest heart's desire, know who I AM. If I know who I am I can be confident enough to do what needs to be done. But at this point Adam, I am lost.

Have you ever wondered why whenever you meet someone, mostly men, you almost automatically identify with the part that's missing on the inside of you? This is especially true for fatherless daughters. While other girls had their fathers to teach order, respect, discipline and structure, we had nothing. Well, that's how we felt anyway. For some of us we feel unloved, looked over, or abandoned. This may be why we are constantly in search mode. We are always looking for the connection that links us with that "missing piece" within ourselves; especially fatherless daughters.

Let's face it; part of our identity is in our father. He is the first man we fall in love with or the first man we hate. We watch how he carries himself so we know what kind of man to choose. Some women have fathers they loved and then he did ungodly things to them, i.e., rape or molestation. How can they find their identity there, when they have nothing but hatred in their hearts? Many others don't know their father. How can a woman love a man she doesn't know? Some girls paint a mental picture of what he may have been like and some block him out altogether. Therefore, the first memory of a father for every little girl is not the same. Sadly, we are left with broken pieces to figure out who we are and what we should do with our lives.

Everything I have read in the Bible concludes that God did not have a verbal conversation with Eve between the time God fashioned her and the moment he placed her in front of Adam.

And the Lord God said, "It is not good that man should be alone; I will make a helper comparable to him." Out of the ground the Lord God formed every beast of the field and every bird of the air, and brought them to Adam to see what he would call them. And whatever Adam called each living creature was its name. So Adam gave names to all the cattle, to the birds of the air, and to every beast of the field. But for Adam there was not found a helper comparable to him. And the Lord caused a deep sleep to fall on Adam and he slept; and He took one of his ribs, and closed up the flesh in its place. The Lord God fashioned into a woman the rib which he had taken from the man, and brought her to the man. The man said this is now bone of my bones and flesh of my flesh; she shall be called Woman, because she was taken out of Man. For this reason a man shall leave his father and his mother, and be joined to his wife; and they shall become one flesh. And the man and his wife were both naked and were not ashamed.

In Genesis 2:18, God did not think it was good for Adam to be alone. God knew Adam needed companionship; though Adam didn't ask for it. Adam was content with what he had been given thus far. He was in constant communion with God! What more could he have needed? God saw that Adam needed a helper and companion! God had given him animals and nature, but there was not any human companionship as there was nothing else like Adam that existed.

God brought each creature to Adam for inspection and identification. This was Adams job! So far, he had been really good at it. He named all the species of animals and had yet to find a helper suitable for himself. Creation was completely named and operating to its highest capacity yet Adam still did not have a companion. Shortly thereafter, God put Adam into a deep sleep, took his rib and fashioned a different creation. WOMAN! Can you believe that several of the creatures we see today were made for Adam as his companion but you are the one that was chosen?

There is no record of God saying anything between fashioning this creation, woman, and taking her to Adam. In the previous text written, he had given Adam the responsibility of giving other species of creation their identity and he would do the same this time around. The being stood in front of Adam and had what I believe was the very first human conversation. If I can imagine for a moment it probably went something like this:

God: Adam! Look what I made! I think we hit the jackpot this time!
Adam: (high fives God) First known praise break. "Lord you are good!" (Queue heavenly praise music)
Adam: (gathers his composure) Hello I am Adam.
Eve: Hello Adam, nice to meet you. Who Am I?

The first human conversation with Adam was one of her unwritten identity. This newly fashioned creation was waiting patiently on her identity and her assignment. She didn't know anything about who she was, where she had landed, where she came from, or where she was going. All the answers depended on what Adam spoke into her existence at that moment. She stood before him and silently received an answer to the 3 questions she did not know she needed answers to and had not yet even asked yet. The conversation continued:

> *Eve: Who Am I?*
> *Adam: WOMAN (at this point Eve was not her name)*
> *Eve: Why Am I here?*
> *Adam: You are my helper. We are to subdue and have dominion over the earth.*
> *Eve: Ok, where do we start? (i.e., what do you need my help doing?)*

In verse 23 Adam tells her where she came from: "this is now bone of my bone and flesh of my flesh". He also told her what she should be "called" which indicated her position. Her name: Woman. Why is she woman? She was taken out of man. Then he finishes with telling her where she is going: "For this reason a man shall leave his father and mother and be joined to his wife and they shall become one flesh." Another instance of Adam giving Eve an identity is when she received the name "Eve" in Genesis 3:20. Again, he assigned her name to dictate her W.A.I. (who am I).

He admonished her and told her she was created to be the mother of all living and Eve simply responded, "OK."

As a woman, this is an all too familiar pattern, but now I understand that it's in our nature. God gave us this inquisitiveness from the very beginning of time. This is how intimate relationships are created. We meet a man and we begin to roll the questions we use to find out who they are while matching them to who we are; well who we think we are anyway. We find a few things in common and call it "compatible". By the end of the first conversation we know things like their career path, family values, and sometimes past hurts. This is all necessary information; however, we use it in a selfish manner. We are in so much pain and have been hurt and broken so much that we choose people who fill our void instead of fuel our future. Many of us don't realize it though. We have been in unhealthy relationships so long that it's "normal".

In many situations today if a woman has been through any type of traumatic situations in her life, such as death of a parent, rape, or molestation she identifies most with feelings of abandonment, rejection, fear and loneliness. When a man comes along that promises to protect her, he is the one! She will do whatever it takes to keep him around. The anxiety and fear of being hurt again is so great that it's worth it to her to keep the protection. She will look past the fact that he's a habitual cheater, unable to commit to anything for long periods of time; living with his momma, or living off of her, and the list goes on. We call this - "love". So next time you choose a mate, think ahead, not behind.

How did I get here? This is the question we so often ask ourselves when we have arrived at a place in life that we are not proud of. Often times I hear, as I am sure you have as well, "your decisions led you here". While that may be true to a degree, some situations that may have been avoided are the result of bad decisions, but some situations were just unavoidable. In either situation it's not necessarily something that we asked for but God saw it as a necessary turning point in our lives. Therefore, there is definitely something to be gained from it.

Situations, circumstances, and a myriad of events happen to us daily. Sometimes we get overlapping troubles while our triumphs seem scarce. Just as soon as we recover from one event, we are faced with something else. The struggle between jobs, family, career, children, husbands, and the like, can have your head spinning with all the things that can or may go wrong on a daily basis.

I am sure you could write a book as well about your story, what terrible "cards" you have been dealt, and how bad people may have treated you along the way. My story may be nothing compared to yours. There are tons of stories in this world about tragedy and how people overcame them. While I hope to inspire you to live again, I also hope to encourage you to action and self-discovery to answer the true question: Who Am I? Once you are able to identify who you are, nothing can ever stand in the way of your defined purpose, destiny, or dreams. You will be able to dream again, live again, and laugh again without fear. You will begin to make choices based on destiny, not fear. When you know who you are and who you belong to the journey gets a lot easier. Who you are has nothing to do with where you are and everything to do with who you belong to.

Life is not about purpose as much as we think it is. It's really about position. The truth is that my location, demographics, age, career, and religious denomination all have the ability to change but not my position in Christ.

Ephesians 2:4 explains this for us:

But God, who is rich in mercy, because of His great love with which He loved us, even when we were dead in trespasses, made us alive together with Christ (by grace you have been saved), ***and raised us up together and made us sit together in the heavenly places in Christ Jesus****, that in the ages to come He might show the exceeding riches of His grace in His kindness toward us in Christ Jesus.*

If I had I known my position in Christ, I would not have made as many bad decisions along the way because of the events that took place in my life. Remember: The tragic events that are out of our control don't have the ability to change who we are.

People will call you everything but a child of God, decide to leave you, walk away from you and that does not change your position. Stay seated in the position that God has given you. No matter if you have been handed the cards of homelessness, divorce, widow, abandonment, rejection, or unemployment, this is ALL temporary! God is the only thing existing that is eternal.

Remember your condition does not change your position. Allow God to elevate you in His perfect timing.

Purpose changes as we evolve as human beings. Our geographical location can change instantly. Tornadoes, fires, hurricanes, and other acts of God beyond our control can change our location instantly! Position will never change. Nothing in this world is able to change who you are. God has called you to be a child of the King. Satan, the father of lies, will tell you differently. He will tell you that since your mother left you, no one will ever love you. Or because you got fired from a job, you are stupid for trying to run your own company. God has made us some major promises in his Word. We just have to know what they are and follow His lead.

I know I have a purpose, but how can I be beneficial to a world that seems to not even want me in it? Every time I turn around something bad is happening. I hear this quite often. In addition, conflict comes because of your purpose and I know that sounds weird, but that's just the way God has this life designed.

I'm sure you have heard it many times and read many books about it. We all want to know our purpose, right? Or do we? I believe it is deeper than that. I believe we are in search of our true identity in a world that offers us everything but the truth. I know I can "do" a lot of things.

An iron serves a "purpose". It is designed to get wrinkles out of clothing. It is made up of many components that enable it to function as an iron. Somebody placed an identity on the iron in order for in to function in its purpose. So wouldn't that mean I need to get my identity from my creator so I know exactly what it is I was created to do? I am more than my personality. I am more than the sum of the things I have learned thus far in my life. I am worth more than the value other people have placed on me. It is for God to show us the W.A.I., not people. Your identity is yours, not somebody else's. There is no way another person can tell you what is on the inside of you. Only God shall reveal that to you in due season.

The Lie Heard Round the World

Historically the phrase "the shot heard round the world" stems from the first shot that was made in a war. Theoretically, no single gunshot can be heard around the entire world. It was the impact of the one shot that was not only heard, but it also affected the present day and the future to come.

This is the same with "the lie heard round the world." This lie shook heaven AND earth. This is the lie that turned humanity for all of eternity. It had angels baffled and even God himself was perplexed. What was the first lie? That we Lack is the first lie.

Adam and Eve already had everything they would EVER need. They had direct access to God. God knew what was best for them and what they would need, and also what they needed to stay away from. Isn't it ironic that we trust God in the times when he is giving things to us, but when he is trying to keep us away from harm we think he is holding something back?

Be very clear, the evil one does his job well. I need you to do yours well. In order to know and operate in who you are you must become fully aware that the accuser will try to convince you that you are not enough, God is not enough, and God is trying to keep something from you. If Satan can convince you of that, you lose and he wins.

Let's go back to the beginning so I can reveal to you how I discovered "the lie heard round the world".

Journey with me to Genesis 3:

Now the serpent was more cunning than any beast of the field which the Lord God had made. And he said to the woman, "Has God indeed said, You shall not eat of every tree of the garden?"

142

and the woman said to the serpent "we may eat the fruit of the
trees of the garden; but of the fruit of the tree which is in the midst
of the garden God has said, "you shall not touch it, lest you die."
Then the serpent said to the woman, "You will not surely die. "For
God knows that in the day you eat of it your eyes will be opened
and you will be like God, knowing good and evil." So when the
woman saw that the tree was good for food, that it was pleasant to
the eyes and a tree desirable to make one wise, she took of its fruit
and ate. She also gave to her husband with her, and he ate.

WHAT! Wait a minute. Are you telling me, that Adam
just had this great conversation with Eve about her identity and
showing her the W.A.I. How they were going to have dominion
over the earth and now this! God just told them they could have
everything BUT the tree of good and evil. He told them if they
didn't do it his way, this would be a BAD, very bad, experience for
them. Up until now there are no counts of Adam and Eve ever
having to feel God's wrath or punishment. Maybe they just didn't
believe the all mighty powerful, peaceful, and loving God would
do anything to harm them? I don't know what they were thinking!
They challenged Gods authority and Satan challenged their
identity. Do you ever find yourself doing the same thing? God has
shown you where he is taking you and Satan is whispering in your
ear; "you are unable to afford it, you are ugly, nobody loves you,
God has left you." He doesn't change.

Adam and Eve's identity had no lack in it because they
were directly connected to the source Himself; God. God had
proved himself to Adam and Eve up until this point. Eve was
birthed out of Adams need! If God can birth a whole person out of
a need, surely he can birth whatever dream or vision he put inside

of you! He is not broke or lacking in anything! There was absolutely nothing they could have needed that God was not able, capable, and willing to give them. They were exactly where they were supposed to be, walking in their God given authority and had direct access to the King! Why did Eve entertain the thought that she didn't have everything she needed? A few answers come to mind.

First, she considered what the father of lies had to say and allowed compromise to enter the equation.

Never for a moment consider anything that the enemy has to say to you. Stop talking to the enemy! Who is your daddy? Is it the father of lies or the Father of Truth? You cannot believe both. God has already promised to give you life more abundantly. It is up to you to choose this day to follow him and never again be persuaded by the evil oppressor to go against the will of God for your life.

Now, one lie is always followed by another. What was the second lie? Shame is the second lie.

Genesis 3:7

Then the eyes of both of them were opened and they knew they were naked; and they sewed fig leaves together and made themselves coverings. And they heard the sound of the Lord God walking in the garden in the cool of the day and Adam and his wife hid themselves from the presence of the Lord God among the trees of the garden. Then the Lord God called to Adam and said to him, "Where are you?" So he said, "I heard Your voice in the garden, and I was afraid because I was naked; and I hid myself."

Isn't it funny that we still do this today? Well, it's not really funny at all. It is very painful and exhausting and it goes back to the "poker face" chapter. Adam and Eve knew they messed up. How? They had been experiencing life the same way every single day but this was different. They had been uncovered and they knew it; though they had never experienced "naked" before. Whatever they were feeling, experiencing or seeing was not good. If it had been then they would have been basking in it when God came looking for them.

God knew they had gotten out of position. He knew that they had changed locations without his permission - spiritually and physically. They didn't even look the same. They had created something to cover themselves in an effort to hide as they were ashamed. Their confidence in God as their covering was no more. Why was God no longer good enough to be their covering as he had always been?

When we participate in the believing the lies of lack and shame we become our own gods. We begin to think it is up to us to provide for ourselves, cover ourselves and ultimately rely on ourselves. This is why shame is sin because it is a lie. The deceiver wants to make us believe that we serve a God who is not forgiving. Our true identity in Christ reveals that our position is in Christ and not in our actions. However, our actions reflect if we believe in our position in Christ! God gave us a remedy when we feel shame:

They looked to Him and were radiant, and their faces were not ashamed. Psalm 34:5

Forever and always God will be omniscient. God already knows what you lied about and are going to lie about. God needs you to know what the lie is so he can help you deal with it. God cannot effectively change in you what you refuse to confront and be honest about. Choose to accept that you are radiant and give him your shame.

Lastly, the third lie was "Blame".

Genesis 3:11:

*And he said, "Who told you that you were naked? Have you eaten from the tree of which I commanded you that you should not eat?" Then the man said, "The **woman** whom You gave to be with me she gave me of the tree and I ate." And the Lord God said to the woman, "What is this you have done?" The woman said, "The **serpent** deceived me, and I ate."*

So, who was really to blame? Who was really at fault? The man said the woman, the woman said the serpent but nobody said "God **I** went against what you told me to do and **I** ate it because I wanted to". God knew they had to have been influenced by something else. He wanted to see how true to themselves they would be. My grandmother used to tell me "every tub sits on its own bottom". As a child I didn't understand this. The explanation that I can now give is that each of us is responsible for ourselves and we are ultimately responsible for our own actions. Nobody will be there to constantly take the blame for what you chose to do but you.

Blame will constantly point the finger at the other person or thing that is causing our reaction. Yes, there are events that occur that we have no control over, but there are tons that we have absolute control over. Yes, we are offered ideas and temptations of all kinds from the enemy but that doesn't make it his fault. If you choose your decision from a place of authority and power and not from a victim mentality you will get much further. We have got to train ourselves to stick with our identity.

In the beginning Eve reminded the deceiver of what God had said. However, he wore her down. Her position didn't change; she changed her mind about how she saw God and how she saw herself. Don't allow the enemy to come in and cloud your judgment of God or yourself. The enemy lied to me when I was 13 years old. He told me that I wasn't pretty enough, when I was 16 he told me, I wasn't good enough and when I was 18 he told me settle, this is all you can get anyway. When I was 20 he told me, I couldn't be a good mother. When I was 25 he told me I was stupid because I got married when God told me not to. He told me countless times that nobody would want to be with me because I was too much to handle. He also said that God would never forgive me for getting a divorce.

When I was 30 he told me, give up just go back to living like a heathen. Then when I was 33, I finally opened my mouth and boldly declared to Satan: "NO more lies Satan! I REFUSE to believe or receive anything other than what God promised me! I am the righteousness of God in Christ Jesus. I am seated with him in heavenly places. I have all authority and power that I need to put you in your place. So right now you have no more authority to trample throughout my life. Go back to hell where you came from!"

What lie has Satan spoken over your life that needs to be cancelled?

Lights! Camera! Action!

"Lights! Camera! Action!" Traditionally, this is another common phrase that you will hear from the director if you were to go behind the scenes of the filming of a television show, commercial, or movie. The director often shouts these words out to the crew as they prepare the actor(s), lighting crew, and sound techs for what is to come next. Keep in mind, it depends on what it is being filmed; be it television, movie, or commercial that will determine how much preparation went into that moment. An actor appearing in a commercial may not need to practice as long as an actor who is in a movie. Both actors, regardless of how many lines they have to deliver, still have to give 100 percent participation to study, apply, and deliver. Have you ever wondered why they shout Lights! Camera! And then Action? Why don't they just say action? What would happen if they said something random like "let's go"?

Somewhere, somebody knew that we needed direction in order to know how to prepare to move forward. This is where you are in life. This is your season of preparation. I believe the reason they shout those words is because they have to set up what is to happen next and get everyone on the same page. Directors are aware of the intricate details that go on behind the scenes which have to take place before the action. Listen closely for the voice of your heavenly father to start showing you and directing the scenes of your life!

Set your mind (focus) on things above, not on things on the earth. Colossians 3:2

Action!

What if the actor never prepared for his lines? Or maybe he knew his lines but when it was time for "Action!" he was busy watching what the camera guy, or the lighting team, were doing? Now several could argue what the most important part of this line would be - Lights, because without them you are blind to what exist past the darkness or Camera, because you must focus and capture the images. Although individually, they each carry a lot of weight, Action is the most important part of this phrase. Why? Because, without action you are just wasting power and there is nothing but electricity that has been wasted if the actor has not taken time to study and prepare for this moment. This is his moment! He was given time to prepare and the proper tools.

Any director will tell you time is money. Would you still watch a movie if everybody was holding a script in their hands? You would not be able see their faces because they were all flipping through their pages trying to find their lines in the script. If an actor comes on the set unprepared everybody else might as well go home. It's just a waste of time. Be prepared when God calls for you to display the gifts that He has put inside of you.

First plant (prepare) your fields; THEN build your barn.
Proverbs 24:27msg

T.A.G

"Tag! You are it! It's your turn!" Remember the childhood game, Tag? Where you ran around with two or three of your friends tirelessly until you could chase somebody down and once you tapped them it was their turn to run? This is where you are in life! TAG! It's your turn! Take Action Girl! God has set the stage for your life. Remember, you don't have to worry about finding an external lighting source for the lights on the set of your life. Matthew 5:14 says, you are the light.

You are the light of the world. A city set on a hill cannot be hidden; nor does anyone light a lamp and put it under a basket, but on a lamp stand, and it gives light to all who are in the house. Let your light shine before men in such a way that they may see your good works and glorify your father who is in heaven. (NASB)

I stress that point twice because often we feel as if we need something external to help us do what God has called us to do. EVERYTHING YOU NEED TO CONQUER THIS WORLD IS ALREADY IN YOU!

You are of God, little children, and have overcome them, because He who is in you is greater than he who is in the world.
I John 4:4

God will light your path. He will guide you and will often bring others to help illuminate your path. Even in situations where God has required us to walk alone for a season there is enough power in us to light our own path!   This is an extraordinarily powerful revelation.   So many times people try to convince us that we need them to complete the vision God has given us. If God says that I am the light, then I have the power to clear out any darkness that surrounds me without any additional help!

The cameras in our lives help us find focus in this busy world. Yes, we can physically find a focus point when walking just by looking with our natural eyes. You are naturally created to follow what your eyes show you. However, in Matthew 6:6 Jesus says,

Here's what I want you to do: find a quiet secluded place so you won't be tempted to role-play before God. Just be there as simply and honestly as you can manage. The focus will shift from you to God, and you will begin to sense His grace.

Go past your natural ability to see. It is in this place that we focus on what or rather who really matters, God. God will bring the lens of your life into focus. He will not only show you who he is, but he will show you who you are and what you should be doing right now. Our world is so busy and we can get caught up doing a lot of unnecessary things. Even if it's good, doesn't mean it is of God. It is in times of uncertainty that we need to go into this quiet place and seek Gods answers. When we pray He will bring our lives into focus so that when He yells Action! We will be ready.

And Action! Are you ready? I mean really ready? Are you prepared for what God is showing you? Have you gained as much knowledge as you could on the subject matter of your destination? Have you researched where you are going? Have you sat with the Father to receive your instructions? Or have you sat in a place of pity and despair because you couldn't figure out what is going to happen next? Are you still angry because of where you are in life or what got you here? Cancel those negative thoughts now. This is a mental attack of the enemy. Satan is attempting to place discouragement on your heart so that you will not finish what God showed you. God didn't change his promise because of the challenging circumstances. You are exactly where you are supposed to be. Try this, instead of waiting on the next bad thing to happen, expect a blessing. Expect the next miracle that God is going to perform through you and for you. Sister, you already have it in you! Don't take my word for it, take God's.

I've written to warn you about those who are trying to deceive you. But they are no match for what is embedded deeply within you- Christ anointing, no less! You don't need any of their so-called teaching. Christ anointing teaches you truth on everything you need to know about yourself and him, uncontaminated by a single lie. Live deeply in what you were taught. I John 2:27

Many people get stuck here. They find themselves stuck in the mindset that it will never happen for them. This verse tells me that we have exactly what we need as long as we abide in Him. It is absolutely true that some seasons are longer than others and sometimes it looks as if nothing is happening. Trust me! There are times I feel the same way! However, it is in this place of preparation that God is working behind the scenes on your behalf. Don't forget, TAG! You ARE it! It's time for change. Be the change you want to see. Only you and God know what areas of your life are broken and need mending. You are the change you seek! Sister, you have to prepare. You must decide now: It's up to me to use all these gifts God placed inside of me. God will show me the W.A.I, he will show me how, and in return I will be obedient.

We have all sorts of reasons why we don't want to walk in the callings God has given us, such as: I'm afraid, What if people don't like me? It didn't work the last time. God is not asking for you to make it happen. He said do the work. Its action time! It's time out for waiting for someone else to manifest the blessing that God promised for you. I know there are times that giving up may seem like the only option, but trust me, God always has another way.

Now that you know the W.A.I., Who Am I, this should no longer be a burden. It will bring you pure joy knowing that you are not alone; you are exactly where you are supposed to be, doing what God put you on this earth to do! You no longer have to wait on anyone to confirm or affirm who you are or get their permission to act on what God spoke to you.

Free At Last

My stay at the domestic violence shelter lasted a period of 90 days as you cannot stay any longer than that. You can come back if the situation arises but, you have to leave and return at a later date. There were women who had been there 3 and 4 times. My heart really cried out for them. Some returned because they had nowhere else to go, others went back to their abusers, and well you can imagine the rest.

As I began to end my stay at the shelter, I had no idea where I was going to live. I still had a job but I didn't have any transportation or housing. What was I going to do? Well I sure wasn't going to say how broke, or poor or homeless I was. God had taught me how to have faith and walk in victory. I didn't have to wear the mask of shame anymore. If I didn't get a car before I left, God would bring me one in his timing.

God began to answer my prayers as my time drew near to leave. One of my coworkers heard I was looking for housing and she was looking for a roommate! Also, as I didn't have any expenses, I had saved my money the past few months in order to get a car. Though I went to a several car dealers, and was turned down, I still continued to believe. Two days before I was to leave the shelter I received a call from a local car dealer saying that I had been referred to them and wanted to know if I was still in the market for a car. "Why absolutely", I shouted. I went to the car lot and drove off with a car that day! As I went back to the facility I wept. My heart was filled and overjoyed with the new life God had given me.

God showed me HE was the perfect father. He had protected me from danger. He provided everything I needed. He showed me he was the perfect gentleman. He pursued my love and caused me to fall in love with him. Then he opened every door I needed and allowed me to simply walk through it. He performed miracles on my behalf. He PROVED himself to be more than I could have ever asked for in a husband AND father! My poker face was gone. I no longer had to be fake it. I could be ME! I didn't have to put on a façade. God was able to love me right where I was. Heartache, disappointment, anger, abuse and confusion; God knew the whole time that was not the end of my story. As Jeremiah 29:11 reminds us,

I know the thoughts I think toward you, says the Lord, thoughts of peace and not evil, to give you a future and a hope.

God had a plan for my life from the very beginning! This was just a small part of my story. While my journey was definitely not over, I was confident in God that my past was no longer holding me hostage. My faith had been renewed. I knew exactly who I was and to whom I belonged. I realized I served an amazing God, and He was the best Father I could have ever asked for. He was the one who loved me passionately and would never let me go. From now on, no one could ever take that away from me.

As I pulled back up to the facility in my brand new car, several of the women congratulated me. Others wept tenderly as I prepared to leave. Who would have thought God would use me to create such a beautiful atmosphere of sisterhood on the campus of a domestic violence shelter? We stood there for a moment a reminisced about the past 90 days.

One of the times I was reminded of was when one of the ladies was out in the gazebo contemplating suicide. They ran into my room one evening screaming, "Brandy! We need you!" "What you want me to do", I asked in confusion. "You know God, so we need you to come pray NOW!" I ran as fast as I could out to the garden where the gazebo was located. I laid hands on her and everybody else that was out there, and prayed for every woman that was at the facility including the faculty. We began to sing and worship God. The presence of the Lord engulfed that gazebo! Even as I type this tears stream down my face. I remember that moment so clearly. She looked me in my eyes and said, "Thank you for being here. I don't know what I would have done without you. The God in you saved my life." Many of the women had not gone to church in years. However, I was even fortunate enough to have gotten connected to a woman at the facility and her Pastor picked us up in his Hummer each Sunday morning. We were riding in style from the domestic violence shelter to church. God really has a sense of humor.

After that experience, I remembered God reminding me of what he had said when I first arrived to this dreaded facility. "This is your assignment. While you are here, give them more of me'. I was not trying to come here to give them Jesus. Honestly, I was trying to get myself together just like they were. Why would God choose me? I was humbled.

I gave God my defeat and he gave me victory. From then on I believed and so I was Victoria. I wanted everybody to know that even in the face of adversity. God laughs. He knows we have already won. I knew I had finally found my W. A. I.

They would often ask me, "Brandy, why are you so happy? How can you keep going"? My answer was simple, "Because I know this is temporary. God is going to deliver each and every one of us. There are good lives waiting for us on the other side if we just hold on and keep pushing forward". They were shocked to hear my answer. I didn't know their individual futures. I am no fortune teller or physic. I just know how BIG my God is!

My roommates even asked if I could teach them to read and understand the bible and how to worship and talk to God! The special moment for me would have been during a car ride to the grocery store. A young lady that accompanied me asked me, "Brandy, can you walk me through being saved"? I said sure, with no hesitation. "When we get back to the shelter, I will be glad to". God immediately stopped me and reminded me that life is not promised and we were not guaranteed to make it back to the shelter. I held her hand and we went through the prayer of salvation right there in the car. Praise God she accepted Jesus right there in the grocery store parking lot!

Be Bold! God can use you in any capacity he chooses! When you are not afraid to be bold and speak up for Him the possibilities of blessings are countless. The women I met at the shelter didn't just end up there by chance. It was by divine assignment that we connected and I am eternally grateful.

I packed my belongings into my new car, said goodbye to the staff and my friends and drove away from the facility with the song in my heart that was sang at my father's funeral:

I'm free, praise the Lord I'm free
No longer bound, no more chains holding me
My soul is resting, it's just a blessing
Praise the Lord
Hallelujah! I'm FREE!

It's just not that I was free FROM the facility. The facility was only a temporary accommodation. I was FREED to something. I was FREED TO BE ME! I was free to be all that God had called me to be. I was no longer bound by the torturing thoughts of failure and defeat. I no longer needed the validation of a man to confirm who God called me to be. I did not have an earthly father, but I did have a heavenly Father who loved me very much! It wasn't about the job or the car; I still did not have back everything that lost. However, I had the one thing that nobody could ever take from me again - My identity in myself and God.

Sister, thank you for spending time with me. Thank you for coming to hear about my journey. What a journey we have been on! I pray something you have read has inspired you to be the real YOU. If anybody can feel your pain, I can. I have been exactly where you are. There is another side to this story. You will not always have to dry your eyes from the tears you cry at night. You will hold your head up again. Your father God in heaven loves you more than you will ever know. Don't be afraid to step out of your comfort zone and speak up for who you are and what you want to accomplish. You are free to be the real you without shame, fear, or hesitation. If you have flaws, and we all do, God will correct them along the way. Just stick close to him. No, the journey does not stop here. We are always on a constant evolving door of change. The greatest thing about revelation is once you know the truth you can no longer be deceived. That doesn't mean you will never be tempted again. As a matter of fact because of this, you can expect something to test your new found belief! But don't look back!

The truth is you may have been dealt a hand you thought you could not handle and you may still be dealing with it today.

Unexpected events happen every day. You are not alone. I hope that something in this book touched you enough to dig a little deeper and discover what actually brings you pain and helps you deal with it! Your life will be much happier once you DEAL WITH IT!

Do not be afraid of the conflict that arises. Do not be afraid of the pain. The conflict is just confirmation you are on the right track. While you are dealing with it, put on the garment of praise and give your spirit of heaviness to God. What good is a life not lived? Live your life the way God intended for you to and not man. God is our Father period. You don't have to be bound in the mistakes of your past. It wasn't your fault that your earthly father was not there to take care of you. Begin to make choices base off of how your heavenly father sees you. You can make a difference in this world.

Life exists in not holding good cards, but only on how we play the hand. - Randy Paush

Play your hand with the understanding that God picked your cards. Your steps were ordered by the Lord and He knows the plans he has for you! No matter what anybody else says about it, you are loved by God, and if that's all you get, it's more than enough.

Lastly, before you can even move forward to freedom, you must first go backward. It is necessary and it is worth it. We are a chosen generation regardless if our natural fathers are here to celebrate with us or not. Deal with the pain so you can get to your purpose. Take the key points of this book with you and live your best life!

1. Forgive your Father (or whomever you hold a grudge against) and let the pain go. It hurts to let it go, but it hurts worse to hold on to it!

2. Forgive God

3. Forgive yourself and free your spirit to love again.

4. Forgive others; they know not what they do.

5. Confront your fears with no option of backing down

6. Love always in spite of circumstances

I will not lie to you and tell you that life is going to get easier. I don't know that "easy" is ever a word that I will use to describe this lifetime. What I do know is that God loves us more than we can ever imagine and we can find our W.A.I in Him! Just like with a GPS he will show us the way, His way. We don't ever have to feel lost again. When you know who you are and who you belong to, pray to your Father and He will make your way clear. Now shout it to the world! I AM FREE! I KNOW WHO MY FATHER IS AND I KNOW WHO I AM!

Dear Daughter,

This is your Father, your Daddy. The one who created your soul before you ever had a body. The one who loves you more than you can ever imagine. I love you very much. I am madly in love with you. I am proud of you. I know this journey has been tough. I sent my son Jesus, not to eliminate your problems, but to help you rise above them. I am with you every step of the way. I am proud of you for being willing to deal with the pain of yesterday, the confusion of the present, and the fear of tomorrow. You have nothing to fear in this world! The hardest part was deciding to deal with it. Now it's time to dive into the process. It will not be easy, but it will all be worth it. You have suffered great losses in your life. I will comfort you and heal you. I promise you will receive recompense, and everything you lost will be restored! You will accelerate forward in healing, power, love, and forgiveness! You have everything you need to make difference in this world. I am here to help you deal with ever heart ache you have. Once you deal with the hand you have been dealt it can no longer hold you in bondage. I am the way the truth and the life. The truth will make you FREE! Be free to live, laugh, love, and enjoy this prosperous life I have given you.

It's a new season! It's a new day! Fresh winds of change are blowing each and every day. I love you with an everlasting love. Don't worry about being rejected. The reasons people reject you are not really about you, it's about the God on the inside of you. When people can't manipulate and control you but rather decide to just leave you and allow you to be your own person, to make your own decisions. Don't concern yourself with who is or is not for you. Your circle is about to change. Get ready to set your bar higher! You can achieve it if you believe it and in the end you will receive ALL that I have blessed you with. Set the BAR higher.

1. Believe It!

2. Act on it!

3. Receive it!

Eternally Yours,
Your Father

Undying Love,
Daddy

Epilogue

Isn't God such a gentleman? He opens doors for us, even writes love letters! If you listen real closely he will whisper sweet, loving, sensitive words in your ear. He will hold you at night and kiss you with His morning sunlight. He will be everything you need. Yes, men are very important and valuable to our existence, but not at the expense of whom we are called to be as individuals. You are not the ultimate sacrifice, Jesus was.

I know firsthand that God is the perfect Father and Husband. He is everything that we believe we missed out on. It's ok to let the anger go for your father not being there, or leaving unexpectedly. Look back over your life. God has always been there! Look closely, at the times you didn't think you were going to have a way out, he made a way. He is the perfect lover, he cares for you. He can heal your wounded soul, but first you have to do the hardest thing. The one thing you have refused to do since you were a little girl. But it's the one thing that will ultimately set your soul free. You must open up. Be vulnerable. Be willing to show your imperfections and flaws. This is where the true healing is. Truth is freedom; Naked before the Lord.

God promises he will cover us with the shadow of his wings. Cover Girl doesn't have a make-up that can cover a wounded soul. Being naked in the presence of the Lord is ok. He promised to be a shield around me. We are safe. This is why the truth makes you free, because you don't have to hide behind the lies anymore! You can walk with your head held high, shoulders back, ready to take on whatever the world has to offer you, without fear! What dreams would you accomplish if you did not have fear of people and their opinions of you holding you back? What attacks of the enemy could you thwart if you only knew the truth about you?

I have walked you through my journey of discovering my issue, dealing with my pain, and soaring into my destiny without pain, fear, bitterness, inhibition, or lack holding me back! Familiarity can be a curse. You must go into the unfamiliar to get healed. It may be uncomfortable for a while, but that's okay. It will get better.

The cards you were dealt in this lifetime were not of your choosing, but what you decide to do about it from here on out is. Be sure to take inventory of ALL your cards, not just pain. God has given us cards of salvation, peace, freedom, deliverance, and healing. So now that you have the key to dealing with the hand you were dealt, the question is: Will you deal with it?

DEAL OR NO DEAL?
THE CHOICE IS YOURS!

Let's Deal with It
Discussion Guide

1. What issues do you believe God is nudging on your heart strings to deal with?

2. List a few ways you will begin to address the issues God has reveal to you.

3. Find you an accountability partner, who will be a constant reminder of your new decisions.

4. Write a letter to your father (and anyone else you need to forgive). Be honest. Tell him how you really feel about him. If you choose you may give it to him.

5. List those whom have made you angry, bitter, and offended. Now speak the names allowed followed by, I forgive you.

6. Write a letter to God, your heavenly Father. Tell him how you really feel about Him and what areas you want to open up to him about. Tell him your deepest secrets.

7. List those whom have made you angry, bitter, and offended. Now speak the names allowed followed by, I forgive you.

8. Document how you feel. If you feel animosity still, it may be deeper. Seek God to show you more details.

9. Pray for those on the list, that they be healed also from the experience.

10. A. Define self-sabotaging

    B. List ways that you are self-sabotaging.

11. A. Define self-love

    B. List ways you do not completely love yourself.

    C. List ways you can implement self-love.

12. Name areas of your life you have neglected to organize. Now put them in order.

13. Write a letter to your pain explaining that you will no longer need, want, or allow it to reside in your body and this is an eviction notice.

14. Write a letter to your future apologizing for neglecting it, and explain what you will do to arrive there.

15. Write down each painful memory of your past and find a scripture that tells your truth.

16. Write a letter to the little girl you once were and introduce her to the "new" you.

17. Write out the vision God has shown you.

18. Now get started!

Prayer of Salvation

I do not take for granted that everyone who picks up this book is saved. At this moment wherever you are if you have not accepted the love and life of Jesus Christ as your personal savior you may do so now. He is our Father! The biggest and best card you have been dealt was the opportunity to make Jesus Christ your Lord and savior. If you choose to receive Him now, he will make your life brand new. Remember he is a gentleman, he will not force his way into your life. He is waiting patiently with his arms stretched wide, ready to receive you, all of you, unconditionally.

Say aloud:

Lord, I repent of my sin. I receive you now as my Lord and savior, Jesus Christ. Come live in me and direct my life through the Holy Spirit. I love you forever and always. Amen

National Resources

National Domestic Violence Hotline
1-800-799- SAFE (7233)
www.thehotline.org

National Alliance on Mental Illness
1-800-950-NAMI (6264)
www.nami.org

National Child Abuse Hotline
1-800-4-A-CHILD (1-800-422-4453)
www.childhelp.org

National Red Cross
1-800-RED CROSS (2767)
www.redcross.org

Salvation Army
www.salvationarmyusa.org

National Suicide Hotline
1-800-273-TALK (8255)
www.suicidepreventionlifeline.org

National Eating Disorders Association
800-931-2237

nationaleatingdisorders.org

Sexual Assault Hotline
800-223-5001

www.nsvrc.org

AAA Crisis Pregnancy Center
800-560-0717

Veterans Crisis Line
800-273-8255

National Center for PTSD
www.ptsd.va.gov

National Abortion Recovery Help
866-482-LIFE (5433)
www.nationalhelpline.org

Miscarriage Support
800-821-6819
www.nationalshare.org

Grief Hotline
800-395-5755
www.griefshare.org

Acknowledgments

To my mother, Sandra, thank you for raising me to be a godly woman. Next to the gift of life, there is no greater gift that you could have given me in this lifetime. I love you forever and always. I know raising us alone was not easy, so thank you. I pray that God will bless you beyond your wildest dreams.

To my father, Roosevelt, thank you for giving me life. Heaven only knows why we only got to spend a few years together before you got your wings. Even in that little time we spent together, you gave me value to always believe in myself and God, and the rest would follow. I hope I have made you proud.

To Timiko and Roosevelt, my siblings, and in-laws Tonya and Lamar I love you very much. We have always stuck together, and we always will, not matter what. Thank you for everything you did to keep me afloat. I pray that I have returned the favor and done well as your sister. I am proud of the both of you. I pray God shower his favor and blessing upon you and your families.

To my baby girl, Aniya, I love you more than words can express. Thank you for loving me back to life. You showed up just in time. No matter where this life takes us, whether we are together or apart know that we will forever and always be tied together in our hearts.

To my aunts Wanda, Alice, Annette, and Uncle Stanley thank you for the love you have shown to us. I lost a father, and you lost a brother. Thank you for being there whenever we called, and even when we didn't.

To my aunts Karen, Gena, Frankie, and my Uncles Mark and Carl (rip), thank you for not letting the streets get the best of me. You prayed and prayed and prayed. After you prayed, you hollered some too! But with good reason I'm sure! But you always prayed and believed in me, so thank you. May God return to you one hundredfold what you have given out.

To my grandparents Lillie (rip) & Frank as well as Ellen(rip) & Roosevelt Sr, thank you for being the rock that held these two families together. You both are silent forces behind the scene. You don't say much, but I still hear the love that resonates from your heart.

To my ENTIRE family far and near, thank you for your love and support throughout the years. I thank God that our family still believes in the power of God, prayer, and family. I love you all.

To Apostles Reggie and Terri Rodgers, "thank you" just seems too short of a phrase to express my gratitude for you. You believed in me, when all hope was lost. You have always helped me to push past the pain of my yesterday and helped me reach my tomorrow. I am a product of your prayers. You are truly my guardian angels.

Tandi and Brandy, those must be fake names right? They even rhyme! Of course they do, cause from day one you have always been the one in sync with the rhythmic chaos I call life. Thank you for always being there for the fun times, and the not so fun times. I probably owe you a new couch as many times as I have needed to sleep on it. I will love you to the end of our lives.

To my BCF(Best Cousin Forever) Shonda, you are the sweetest, most loving, craziest cousin a girl could ever ask for! Thank you for the times we have shared together, and let's drive the world crazy…ok "Brownie!"

To anybody who I have ever rubbed shoulders with, shook hands with, or even just smiled at me when I was having a bad day, to you I say thank you. You never know what somebody is going through. Thank you for doing your part in my life.

Lastly, to my hearts joy, thank you. You helped me to see that I was more than able to finish the task God placed inside of me. Our road was rocky, but I am forever grateful to have met you.

About the Author

Brandy Hunt, resident of Greenville, SC was born to Roosevelt and Sandra Hunt. She is the mother of one daughter, Aniya. In addition to writing, acting, and dancing, Brandy is also pursuing a degree Criminal Justice @ Brown Mackie College in Greenville, SC. Brandy is passionate about living a purpose filled life and is committed to help others do the same. She considers herself adventurous, loving, and determined.

"As long as I have lived I have always hated injustice, but now I hate enough to do something about it."

-Brandy M. Hunt

Made in the USA
Charleston, SC
06 March 2015